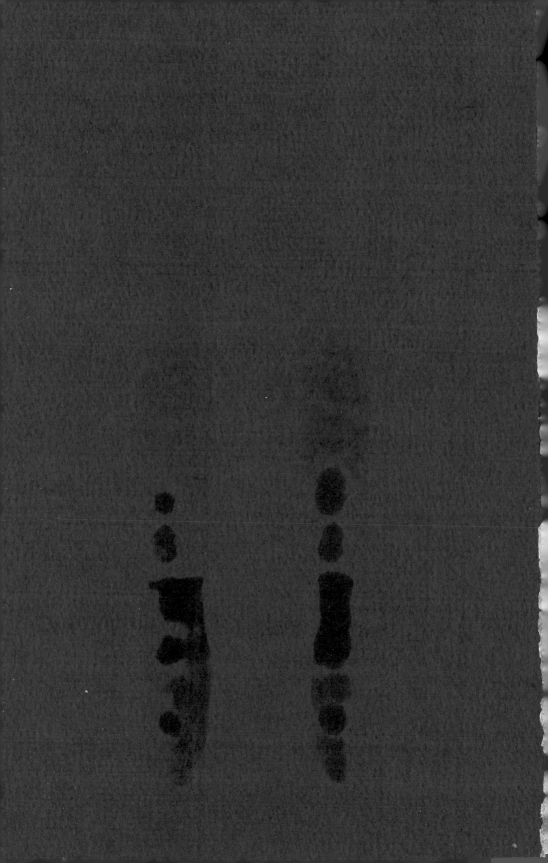

AMERICAN CHARCUTERIE

IN COLLABORATION WITH

JAMES "CHOOCH" POTENZIANI

& ARAYAH JENANYAN

■

VIKING

AMERICAN CHARCUTERIE

▪▪▪▪▪▪▪▪▪▪▪▪▪▪▪▪▪▪▪▪▪▪▪▪

RECIPES FROM PIG-BY-THE-TAIL

▪▪▪▪▪▪▪▪▪▪▪▪▪▪▪▪▪▪▪▪▪▪▪▪

VICTORIA
WISE

VIKING

Viking Penguin Inc., 40 West 23rd Street,
New York, New York 10010, U.S.A.
Penguin Books Ltd, Harmondsworth,
Middlesex, England
Penguin Books Australia Ltd, Ringwood,
Victoria, Australia
Penguin Books Canada Limited, 2801 John Street,
Markham, Ontario, Canada L3R 1B4
Penguin Books (N.Z.) Ltd, 182–190 Wairau Road,
Auckland 10, New Zealand

First published in 1986 by Viking Penguin Inc.
Published simultaneously in Canada

Grateful acknowledgment is made for permission to
reprint the following recipe: "Champagne Sausage"
from The Chez Panisse Cookbook by Alice Waters.
Copyright © 1982 by Alice L. Waters. Reprinted by
permission of Random House, Inc.

LIBRARY OF CONGRESS CATALOGING IN PUBLICATION DATA
Wise, Victoria.
American charcuterie.
Bibliography: p.
Includes index.
1. Cookery, International.   2. Cookery (Meat)
3. Cookery—California—Berkeley.   4. Pig-by-the-Tail
(Berkeley, Calif.)   I. Potenziani, James.   II. Jenanyan,
Arayah.   III. Title.
TX725.A1W57   1986   641.5'09794'67   85-40555
ISBN 0-670-80843-1

Printed in the United States of America by
The Book Press, Brattleboro, Vermont
Set in Goudy Old Style
Design by Liney Li

I would write on the lintels of the door-post, *Whim.*

—Ralph Waldo Emerson

For my parents

FOREWORD

■ ■

F or more than a decade, Berkeley, California, has been the center of the "food revolution" that has swept across the nation. At the nucleus of this phenomenon stands a very modest lady who was the first chef at Chez Panisse restaurant in Berkeley—Victoria Wise. Her pâtés, terrines, galantines, sausages, preserved meats, and cold dishes represent some of the best examples of that revolution: an uncompromising and relentless striving for the very best in quality and taste, and the search for the essence of good food. Starting with the finest raw ingredients, then using age-old classic techniques with improvisation, and, finally, relying on her fine palate, Victoria creates some of the best charcuterie in this country.

I met Victoria through the magical aromas of her charming Pig-by-the-Tail charcuterie many years ago. I had just come back from a year of living and studying in France. My longing to recapture the earthy taste of good French food led me naturally to her. I would often bicycle to her charcuterie while shopping for my cooking classes. But it really was an excuse to taste Victoria's wonderful creations. Although her original inspiration is French, I would unhesitatingly testify that Victoria's food is unique. Like many good cooks in America, she has learned from the diversity of American culture. It shows in her food. From Armenian lamb pizza to Chinese chicken salad, Victoria's imaginative range is limited only by her good taste.

For years I felt that Pig-by-the-Tail should be shared with the rest of the world. It is too good to be kept a secret for Berkeley. After all, it's only fair that others should share—isn't that what food is all about? So, now Victoria and her collaborators have put together an inviting cookbook of their favorite recipes. It is an impressive range of different types of food united by what I believe food should be: simple, honest, tasty, and earthy. These are recipes that make you hungry before you cook and give you enormous pleasure as you prepare them. Like me, you will feel the heady and sensuous aromas. Then you will see why I have such a passion for Victoria's food.

KEN HOM
Berkeley, California
1985

PREFACE

The question most often asked me is, how did you come to start a charcuterie? With a little encouragement, I might revel in memories of the wonderful sensations of sight, smell, taste, and creative energy elicited by my first introduction to charcuterie in France in 1967. On a practical level, I can cite the conflict between my motivating passion to cook, and my dislike of working at night. Charcuterie neatly accommodated both these considerations. It also accommodated my inclination toward the alchemical aspect of cooking: bringing together both the science (understanding chemical reactions in food composition) and the art (creating aesthetic reactions through food composition) of cuisine. Charcuterie held for me then, and it still does today, the fascination of an alchemy that works.

These various motives came together in the place of a small shop, just the right size at just the right time, on the sunny side of the street and at a reasonable price. The timely British publication of Jane Grigson's *The Art of Charcuterie and French Pork Cookery,* which I had purchased at Foyle's in London on that same enlightening European sojourn, provided an accessible guideline. So, in the summer of 1973, armed with determination and a lot of energy, my dear friend and original partner, Barbara Haugeland, and I rented the premises and opened Pig-by-the-Tail, probably the first traditional French-style charcuterie in the United States.

That was a good starting point. The original vision, strong enough to be a sensation before the fact, was that we would shop, cook, serve, sell, keep the records, and clean in a well paced and rational manner which would provide us with both a respectable business and a joyous existence. In the true pioneering spirit of youth, and to save money,

Barbara and I had decided to do the remodeling work ourselves. We hammered and sawed, sheetrocked and laid linoleum, jackhammered and threaded gas pipe. We were nearly finished, and proud of ourselves, when the first moment of conflict between our well arranged dream and the reality of running a shop came to us. After a week of arduous oomphing with heavy pipes, the gas line tested faulty. We had not been strong enough to tighten the joints properly, and gas was leaking all down the line. We broke down and hired a plumber to finish the job so we could start cooking.

One morning, a long three months later, we opened the refrigerator door and a huge bowl of blood sausage mixture—hastily stored the night before in the last available space, right on top of an equally huge bowl of brioche dough—came splattering and flooding out all over us and the floor. If we had not been so exhausted the previous night, we would not have left the blood sausage unfinished; if we had had more experience, we would have known that brioche dough rises, even when refrigerated. Laughing, crying, and cursing, we cleaned up the mess, and revising our original scenario of a two person show, we decided to expand our staff.

The idea of charcuterie was already somewhat familiar in Berkeley, a town full of well traveled people. North Berkeley, which enjoyed excellent food shopping for meats, produce, cheese, and coffees and teas, attracted a clientele looking for a village type marketing atmosphere. The addition of a French delicatessen made our neighborhood a natural center for the burgeoning food culture of the Bay Area in the 1970's. Word of mouth and foot traffic brought us customers, and soon the media was interested in the curious shop full of wonderful food-to-go.

Still, a pork shop was an anomaly in those early years, and an occasion for a number of amusing responses from the not quite certain public: the person who wanted to know if we made our mayonnaise with pork fat; the lady who asked, would we just mind changing the name to something besides "Pig" for the ad we had agreed to purchase in her B'nai B'rith newsletter. Most people thought all pâté was made with liver, that all sausage was made with nitrate, that the celery root *rémoulade* was noodle salad, and who in the world could pronounce *ratatouille*?

Through the years, along with expanding the operation of our shop has come expansion of our concept of charcuterie. Charcuterie began as the profession of preparing pork and other meats. It was extended in one direction to include the right to butcher pork. In the other direction, imaginative *charcutiers* (or was it the *charcutières*?) added composed dishes and accompaniments to their take-out menus. As it developed, classical

French charcuterie became the art and science of cooking and preserving mainly pork products, from pork butchery to take-out cookery.

Depending on the style of the region and the size of the village, French charcuteries today may or may not offer pastries, condiments, and side dishes. Charcuteries in small country towns, such as Revel in the southwest, concentrate on hams, terrines, and sausages, with perhaps a jar of tiny tarragon flavored pickles, called *cornichons,* to round out the bill of fare. Charcuteries in bourgeois towns, such as Amboise in the Loire, vend, in addition to a wider range of prepared pork products, a variety of take home dishes, including quiches, *bouchées à la Reine,* and cooked jumbo artichokes. In Paris, the bill of fare is expanded to include elaborate presentations of eggs or vegetables in shimmering aspics, glistening steamed *langoustines,* and prepared snails ready to pop into the oven.

At Pig-by-the-Tail, in line with contemporary taste, nutritional considerations, and cooking and storage techniques made possible by modern refrigeration, we have lightened up the richness of traditional charcuterie by reducing fat and salt. We have also eliminated preservatives in most dishes, including our fresh sausages. Instead of relying primarily on pork, we have emphasized composed salad dishes using chicken, vegetables, and fish.

The emphasis on fresh salads is, I think, a major contribution of American delicatessen fare to the very old art of charcuterie. "Fresh" and "seasonal" are bywords of what is currently referred to as *nouvelle* California cuisine, and composed salads are its hallmark dishes. Of course, fresh and seasonal have always been precepts of good regional and indigenous cuisines, the opposite of fancy, forced, or false. What is new here is variety, both in number of dishes and of ingredients used. American charcuterie stretches beyond pork cookery to encompass all themes of take-out cookery. The only limits to creativity are that the dish must be at its best even if cold, and that it look as good at home, picnic, or party as it did in the shop.

Our book began, in the first place, as an effort to present the repertoire of Pig-by-the-Tail charcuterie, which is by now too large, and also too seasonal, to array in our physical space at one time. I hope it finishes by offering a small part of culinary enlightenment and a large part of inspiration to its readers: professional, amateur, and armchair cooks alike.

VICTORIA WISE
Berkeley, California
July 1985

ACKNOWLEDGMENTS

I wish to thank, first of all, Stuart Dreyfus, without whose belief in me Pig-by-the-Tail might have remained a fond imagining; and secondly, my collaborators Chooch Potenziani, chef at Pig-by-the-Tail, and Arayah Jenanyan, manager and *sous* chef at Pig-by-the-Tail, without whose tireless dedication to this project in all its creative and technical details, the book would not have been written.

I am eternally indebted and grateful to my mentors and teachers: Jane Grigson, whose eloquent writing and recipes were the first foundation of our pâté and sausage repertoire; to Mme. Marie DesChamps, whose love of charcuterie I shared and under whose tutelage at Le Vivoir Restaurant in Sausalito, California, I learned the structure and workings of a professional French kitchen; Roger Gleize, who kindly shared the secrets and techniques of his craft during my brief apprenticeship at his charcuterie in Revel, France; and to Timothy Murphy, Sr., now deceased, who generously taught us how to pump hams, how to tie sausages, and many other tricks of the butcher's trade, even though he could not believe women were doing "this kind of work."

I offer special thanks to Ann Arnold, a brilliant painter with a fine palate, and touch for baking also, who developed most of the items in our Christmas bakery line; who then, for our book, reduced many of her recipes back to "home" size from the large proportions she had worked up to for the shop—until painting claimed all her time; to Lindsey Shere, pastry chef at Chez Panisse Restaurant, Gary Frisvold, of Lenny's Meats, Ron Fujii, of the Produce Center, and Carey Fujii, who have patiently answered questions and shared information and inspiration over the years; to Paul Rude for his research assistance; to my agent, Martha Sternberg, for suffering so many corrective readings of the manuscript; and to my editor, Gerald Howard, whose continuing enthusiasm and encouragement were responsible for this book's being published.

For their support, ideas, criticism, and for their recipes, I wish to thank my friends and colleagues Veronica Aiken, Penny Brogden, Judith Friend, Christine Harris, Florence Hoffman, Susanna Hoffman, Dale Ketter, Alfred Peet, Lisa Rich, Judith Shane, Gail Stempler, Patty Unterman, Alice Waters, and the staff of Pig-by-the-Tail. Finally, I add a very special thanks to my original partner, Barbara Haugeland, and to my husband, Rick Wise.

Acknowledgments

CONTENTS

—————————————————— SAVORIES *237* ——————————————————

xviii
Contents

BASIC INGREDIENTS & TECHNIQUES FOR CHARCUTERIE

■ ■

THE PANTRY

Salt for kitchen use appears in many forms, from large blocks to crystals of various sizes to powdered. The taste will vary, however, not according to the form but according to geography and whether the source is sea or earth. The mines of Cheshire in England, the Adriatic salt marshes at the mouth of the Po, the seacoast of Aigues-Mortes in France, and the salt works of the African desert have all produced salts at one time or another considered to be the best for this, that, or the other usage.

All cooking salts are more or less impure, meaning they are not 100 percent sodium chloride. Rock salt, which is mined from the earth, is 95 percent sodium chloride. Sea salt, evaporated out of sea water, is 98 percent pure. In general, sea salt is the more highly prized for cooking, especially for pickling and curing. In particular, bay salt is the name for the best grade of sea salt; it is obtained when sea water is evaporated by the sun rather than by artificial means. Vacuum salt is purified salt; it is obtained by evaporating a salt solution purified of calcium salts, which can react with meat to bleach the flesh and form a cloudy brine.

Except where *gros sel,* which is sea salt crystals, is specified in the recipe, we use a vacuum processed powdered sea salt, which is quite dense and 99.9 percent pure, with no "medicinal" aftertaste, and which is easily soluble, leaving no unpleasant residue of undissolved grains in the dish or at the bottom of the brine. It is available in bulk in health food stores.

Pepper also varies immensely in taste according to kind and freshness. Pepper amounts in the recipes are for tellicherry black peppercorns, white peppercorns, and coriander seed (sometimes called brown pepper), freshly ground in a hand cranked, box type coffee grinder. This produces a very aromatic peppering of slightly coarser than usual texture.

Fresh chilies referred to in the recipes are either the long, green (or sometimes red) kind called Anaheims, which may not be hot at all, their

Chilies

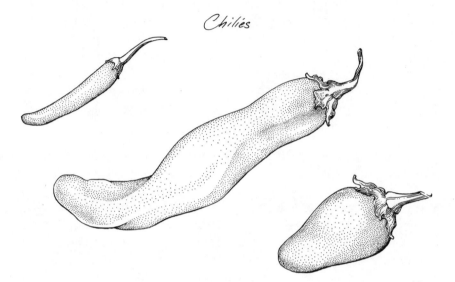

flavor being somewhere between a hot chili and a bell pepper; or the small, usually green (but sometimes red) jalapeño chilies or a close cousin, Fresno chilies. Jalapeños and Fresno chilies range from not too hot to rather hot. Occasionally, we use the small, red serrano chilies or the very small red chilies called *chilitos* (sic!) in Chinese markets, both of which are quite hot. All these chilies provide aromatic hotness which, however, does not linger on the palate even when there is quite a bite. They are not like the hot black chilies of Hunan cuisine or, the hottest I've ever tasted, the beautiful little Caribbean chilies which range in color from yellow through orange to red. Beguiled by their lovely bright colors, I bought a quantity before I discovered their relentless heat, which burned for hours on the tongue, lips, and hands after one touch to the mouth for an inquiring taste.

Amounts given in the recipes for fresh chilies, garlic, shallots, onions, and herbs may need to be adjusted according to the strength and quality of the particular ingredient, as determined by season, variety, and source of the ingredient.

The **pâté spice** referred to in recipes is our house blend of spices for seasoning pâtés and sausages. It is similar to other sweet and peppery aromatic seasonings such as the French blend, *quatre épices,* or the Chinese 5 spice blend. *Quatre épices,* available in kitchen specialty stores, is a modest substitute for pâté spice. However, it will lend a sweet taste to the dish since it usually includes cinnamon. To make pâté spice, mix together 1 ounce ground black pepper, 1 ounce ground white pepper, ½ ounce ground coriander seed, ½ ounce powdered ginger, ¼ ounce grated nutmeg, and ¼ ounce powdered clove. For best results, use freshly ground spices and store in a tightly sealed jar. Pâté spice is also good with all kinds of chicken dishes.

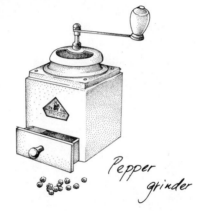

Pepper grinder

MEAT AND FAT FOR PÂTÉS AND SAUSAGES

Most meat ingredients for charcuterie are readily available. Some, like fresh, whole legs of pork to turn into ham or fresh beef tongue to pickle yourself, may not be on display but can usually be ordered in a good butcher shop or even in many modern supermarkets. Chinese and Italian ethnic markets are an excellent source for some of the more esoteric ingredients, such as fatback and duck livers, which are not generally available. Alternatives are mentioned in the descriptions below or in the recipes.

Pork butt (also called **pork shoulder** or Boston butt), which is the upper shoulder of the hog, is the preferred cut for pâtés and sausages.

Quality and price vary throughout the year. The best meat is firm and rosy pink, neither pale (too young) nor as dark rose as beef (too old), and well marbled with fat. It is available in the Fall and through the Spring. Summer pork, which is immature meat, can be quite expensive and is usually flabbier meat, which produces softer textured pâtés and sausages. The cook's judgment is involved in deciding if the material at hand is a bit too lean or a bit too fat, and adjusting the quantity of added fat accordingly. This is a matter of both taste and experience.

As they usually appear in butcher shops and supermarkets, pork butts are already trimmed of excess fat and neatly tied. Weights given in the ingredient lists are for optimal quality trimmed butts. If you purchase bone-in, untrimmed, and untied butts, the fat trim and bone will amount to about 1/3 pound each.

Ground pork from the butcher or grocery store is not as satisfactory for pâté and sausage making, but it may be used if a meat grinder is not part of your *batterie de cuisine*. In this case, the fatback in the list of ingredients for grinding should be reduced by 1/4 pound per pound of pork to compensate for the extra fat in purchased ground pork.

Caul fat is the most unusual ingredient in charcuterie. In its widest sense, caul means any netting used for wrapping. In its anatomical sense, caul is the lacy fat membrane enclosing an organ or other body part. The caul enclosing the lower stomach of a pig or cow is used in charcuterie to line terrines and wrap sausages, providing a protection against drying as it melts during cooking.

Unfortunately for the home cook, caul fat, which was formerly known in American butcher shops as veil fat, is virtually unheard of in retail markets today. Also, it is packed and shipped by slaughterhouses in 20 to 50 pound boxes, so it will take some charming to convince your butcher to carry it unless you want to order a whole box. When caul is unavailable, terrines may be lined with fatback or one of its alternatives (see below) and sausages may be shaped into patties without a wrapping.

Caul fat is quite perishable and should be kept frozen until ready to use. Since it does not refreeze well, wrap and freeze in small packages. To use, defrost and rinse in cold water mixed with a few drops of vinegar to remove the odor. Squeeze out and trim away large globules of fat which won't melt down during cooking and are unsightly.

Fresh, unsalted **fatback,** also called barding fat and speck, is the fat from the pig's back. Sliced into thin rectangular sheets, it is wrapped around meats, such as veal roasts, to provide fat basting during cooking, so it is generally available in butcher shops. It is the preferred fat for adding to pâtés and sausages because it sets up well after cooking, providing succulence without flabbiness. The outside fat from untrimmed pork loin or pork butt can substitute for fatback which is to go through the grinder, although it is less satisfactory for lining terrines than neat square slabs of thick fatback.

Salt pork can substitute for fatback in sausages, but does not work well in forcemeat for pâtés because it is too soft and will produce a flabby texture. Salt pork must be blanched before using: rinse well, remove the rind, and simmer in plenty of water for 15 minutes. Remove, pat dry, and chill several hours. Chill under a weight to keep it from curling if it is to be sliced for lining terrines.

Fatback and salt pork should be weighed after the rind, or skin, is removed. The **trimmed rind** may be cut into squares or strips and made into cracklin's for a salad garnish: cook in a 250 degree oven 4 hours, or until quite crisp. Drain on paper toweling and use warm or store in an airtight container up to 3 days and reheat to use.

The **fat trimming** from pork butts, fatback, or other pork cuts should be melted down, or rendered, to make a long lasting lard, for use in pastry crusts, for sealing terrines, and as a frying medium. To render lard, dice fat into ¼ inch cubes and place in a small, heavy pot with enough water to cover the bottom of the pot. Cover the pot, place on stove top over a metal trivet, and cook over very low heat 5 hours, stirring occasionally. Cool slightly and strain through cheesecloth into a storage container. Three pounds of fat trimming will yield 5 to 6 cups of lard. Refrigerated, lard will keep indefinitely. Duck, chicken, or goose fat trimming may be rendered in the same way.

SAUSAGE CASING

The most familiar sausage casing is natural gut, the intestine of sheep, pig, or cow. **Sheep casing,** which is used for thin links, is the most difficult to manipulate because of its narrow diameter. It is packed in 100 yard **hanks** and is about ½ inch wide. **Hog casing,** the most regular size for fresh sausage, is packed in 100 yard **bundles** and is 1 to 1½ inches in diameter. **Beef casing,** 1½ inches in diameter or larger, is packed in 150 foot **sets** and is used for medium size salamis and large boiling sausages such as *saucisson à l'ail.* Large salamis, bologna, and mortadella are stuffed into **beef bungs,** the large part of the intestine, about 5 inches in diameter, or **beef bladders,** 5½ to 7 inches in diameter. Salt packed, vacuum wrapped sausage casings are often available from butcher shops or delis that make fresh sausages.

Of course, 100 yards of casing will hold far more sausage than a home cook would make at a time; fortunately, refrigerated salt packed casings will keep indefinitely. Once the salt is rinsed off, float the casing in a little water and store in the refrigerator for up to 1 month. Freezing is not a good way to store casings as it breaks down the membrane. As a result, holes form when the casing is filled.

EQUIPMENT AND TECHNIQUES

Equipment for doing the recipes in this book can be found in good kitchenware boutiques or mail ordered through the Williams-Sonoma catalogue, P.O. Box 7456, San Francisco, California 94120-7456. Essential **tools** are an 8 or 10 inch **chef's knife** and a **paring knife.** We prefer stainless steel knives as they are easier to clean and don't blacken vegetables such as onions and eggplant as they cut. Most of the recipes can be prepared in a home kitchen with just these knives, especially if you have a butcher or good supermarket where you can purchase salt pork, fatback, and ground pork, veal, and lamb, and where boning and slicing services are available. For the serious *charcutier,* an **8 inch boning knife,** preferably curved, is necessary for preparing many of the meats for charcuterie.

Other useful tools for doing the recipes in this book are an **instant reading meat thermometer,** several **colanders** and **sieves** of various sizes, a metal stovetop trivet for maintaining even, low heat, and a *batterie* of **pots** and **pans** including one or two 10 to 12 quart pots, a 10 inch diameter and a 12 inch diameter sauté pan, and a 2½ inch to 4½ inch deep sauteuse or casserole. These should be made of a nonreactive material—stainless steel, enamelware such as Creuset brand, or heat processed cast iron, such as Calphalon brand. In the text, we specify using a nonreactive cooking vessel either to avoid the unpleasant metallic taste resulting from the reaction of certain foods with tin, aluminum, or cast iron, or to avoid undesirable color changes, as when egg based sauces turn green if made in an aluminum or cast iron pot.

A **food processor** is a handy, but not essential, **machine aid,** used primarily for making sauces and pâtés which are to have a smooth and homogeneous texture. In addition, an **electric tabletop mixer,** such as a Kitchen Aid brand, with both a **meat grinder** and a **sausage stuffer attachment,** is a most useful machine aid for charcuterie, especially for filling sausage casings. A sausage stuffing attachment to a hand operated meat grinder will do, with a little practice at turning the crank while both feeding the stuffer and manipulating the casing (an extra pair of hands is a help). With determination and patience, a wide mouth, wide tube funnel may be used to fill hog or beef casings, but it is close to impossible to fill the small sheep casings through a funnel.

Grinding is the best method for cutting meats and fats into small but still discrete elements without mashing them. An inexpensive manual grinder with a sharp blade and three plates—small ($\frac{1}{8}$ inch), medium ($\frac{3}{16}$ inch), and large ($\frac{3}{8}$ inch)—will do the job well. A meat grinding attachment to an electric tabletop mixer will make the job easier and faster. If you lack a meat grinder, ingredients that are to be ground medium or coarse may be chopped by hand with a chef's knife instead. Ingredients to be ground fine or puréed may be chopped in a food processor.

When grinding ingredients for pâtés and sausages, fat should be put through last to push the other ingredients through. Gristle and nerve fibers that get caught between blade and grinder plate should be discarded: they will make the forcemeat tough. When processing ingredients in a blender or food processor, pick out and discard stringy fibers that the processor has not been able to cut before seasoning and mixing forcemeat. When hand cutting meats, discard gristle and nerves that the knife cannot cut through.

STOCKS

It is sensible to make thrifty use of meat, poultry, and vegetable trim by brewing up a stock. Stocks, one of the few items we advocate freezing, will keep this way indefinitely, remaining handy for a last minute light soup first course or base for a hearty soup main course. Pork stock, a lot of which can be made as a by-product of charcuterie, is an excellent base for quick Oriental style soups or more substantial dishes such as gumbo and posole. Using the following casual method, the cook doesn't have to worry about saving bones and trimming until there is enough to "make it worthwhile." Start with a small batch and keep frozen until more bones and trimming are available. To expand the quantity, melt down the stock you already have, add new bones and trimming to it, and continue as follows. This procedure will, incidentally, strengthen the stock since stock replaces much of the water in the recipe below.

To make meat or poultry stock, place bones and trimming in a pot. If you like, add a few herbs and vegetable seasonings such as garlic, celery, carrot, onion, mushroom stems, or tomato. To avoid a too salty soup or sauce, no salt should be added until the stock is used in its final form. Cover the ingredients with water by 2 inches and bring just to a boil. Reduce the heat to maintain a gentle simmer, partially cover, and cook 1½ hours for poultry stock, 3½ hours for meat stocks. Skim from time to time. Do not allow to boil or fat will emulsify in the liquid and result in a cloudy stock.

Allow stock to cool slightly, then strain into a storage container and let cool to room temperature. Refrigerate overnight, uncovered. Next day, skim fat off the top, cover, and freeze. To avoid souring by trapped warm, unmoving air over the surface, it is important both to cool the stock before refrigerating and to refrigerate it uncovered until chilled through.

QUANTITIES

The number of people served, or the amount a recipe makes as indicated at the top of recipes, varies according to the dish and how it is to be used. For example, where the indication is "dinner for 4 or a buffet platter for 8," this means four hungry people will consume the dish if it is the main course for dinner, but it can be stretched to serve eight generously on a buffet table where there is one other main dish and perhaps three side dishes. In figuring how far a pâté will go, we allow 1 ounce per person for cocktail parties over 100, and 1½ ounces per person for parties under 100 people. If the pâté is to be served for luncheon or as a first course for dinner, we allow 2½ to 3 ounces per person.

TERRINES, PÂTÉS & GALANTINES

N o matter how unpretentious and simple nor how fancifully adorned, terrines, pâtés, and galantines are basically composed of a **forcemeat** cooked in some sort of wrapping. Forcemeat, called *farce* in French, is finely or coarsely chopped, ground, or pureed meat, poultry, or fish, seasoned and bound with egg, cream, bread, or a combination of the three. It may be layered with strips or pieces of meat, livers, sweetbreads, fat, vegetables, or truffle to vary color, texture, and taste. The wrapping may be caul fat, fatback, bacon strips, salt pork, pastry crust, fish fillets, grape leaves, or, as sometimes in the case of galantines, the skin of the animal.

Terrines, named for the (originally) terra cotta container in which a forcemeat was cooked, range from a simple meat loaf, such as pâté maison, to more complicated dishes, such as *terrine de poissons*. Terrines are baked sitting in a 2 inch hot water bath, called a **bain-marie.** The water steams and keeps the oven air moist during cooking.

Pâtés, precisely speaking, are forcemeat compositions enclosed in pastry crust. The crust, serving the same purpose as a *bain-marie*, seals in moisture released from the meats during cooking. In this book, the words **pâté** and **terrine** are used interchangeably as they recently have come to be in general culinary usage.

Galantines, strictly defined, are boned, stuffed, and shaped meats or poultry poached in aromatic stock. Cooled under weight overnight, they are then glazed with a **gelée,** or aspic, made from the stock. We sometimes bake a galantine to produce good color and crisp skin, in which case we omit the traditional aspic coating.

Meats, fats, onions, shallots, and garlic in the ingredient lists for grinding should be **cut** to whatever size is suitable for the grinder, blender, or food processor being used. The texture of the forcemeat will vary according to whether it is ground, hand chopped, or pureed. Alternatives to and reasons for using one method or another are indicated in the recipes.

Basic meat and fats for charcuterie are discussed in the preliminary notes. In addition, if you are grinding **veal** for pâté, purchase veal stew meat, which is the trim from the bottom round or shoulder, or use an end piece from a veal roast. Although veal shank is usually saved for a more prominent use, its meat is very good in pâté. Any large pieces of gristle are trimmed from veal cuts before weighing. Already ground veal, if available, may be used in recipes without altering anything else.

Chicken breasts for grinding are boned but not skinned before weighing. However, to avoid clogging if using a food processor, the skin of chicken is removed for another use and the weight difference is made up with some other fat.

Ham for grinding should be mild and preferably not smoked. It is often included in forcemeat compositions to provide color as well as taste. The nitrate absorbed in curing gives ham its pink color, and it will also lend a rosy hue to other meats with which ham is mixed, especially if the forcemeat is aged overnight before cooking.

Different methods of **mixing** also produce different textural results. We suggest hand mixing ingredients except where a whisk, electric mixer, or food processor is indicated for beating in air to make a fluffier forcemeat, such as for a mousseline or pâté de poulet. Overmixing meats like turkey or duck results in a tough forcemeat.

The container in which a pâté is assembled for cooking, called a **terrine,** may be of glazed pottery, ceramic, ovenproof glass, enamel, aluminum, or tin. Preferences for one container or another are indicated in the recipes.

Besides style of flavoring, one of the things which makes pâtés and terrines different from meat loaf is the procedure of **lining the terrine,** usually with some kind of fat to provide succulent moisture during cooking.

Caul fat is the easiest material to use for lining a terrine. Just drape a large piece (about ⅓ pound) over the terrine, easing it down onto the bottom and into the corners. Cut away excess, leaving enough hanging over the sides to fold over and enclose the pâté. Patch any large holes with the trimming.

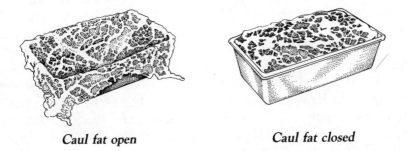

Caul fat open   *Caul fat closed*

Fatback is also particularly suitable for lining a terrine. Because it is hard fat, it will retain its form during cooking and provide an appealing white frame around the pâté slices. It is usually not eaten in this form, although it is edible.

To line a terrine with fatback, cut into slabs 5 by 6½ inches. Chill in the freezer 15 minutes, then slice as thin as possible, preferably ¹⁄₁₆ inch thick, into rectangles the size of the slab. Or purchase barding fat already sliced from a butcher. Choose 5 of the most perfect slices for the bottom, ends, and sides: place one in the middle on the bottom of the terrine. Smooth out, then place another piece slightly overlapping at each end of the bottom piece. Smooth up and over ends of the terrine to overhang by 1½ inches. Use an extra piece if necessary. Fill in the sides with slightly overlapping slices of fatback, cutting pieces to fit the shape of the terrine and to overhang edges by 1 inch. Have ready 2 or 3 more pieces to cover the top of the terrine when filled. Place them, slightly overlapping, to within ½ inch of the sides and 1 inch of the ends. Fold up overhanging edges to enclose neatly.

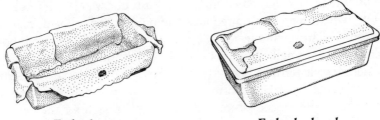

Fatback open   *Fatback closed*

Salt pork and **bacon** are readily available materials which may be substituted in recipes calling for fatback or caul fat to line a terrine. However, both of these should be blanched and chilled first to minimize the addition of their distinctive flavors and excess salt to the pâté.

Unless you want to carry your blanched and chilled salt pork back to the butcher to cut on his slicer, chill in the freezer for 15 minutes, then use a chef's knife to cut as thin as possible into approximately 1 inch by 3 inch rectangles resembling a short piece of bacon. To line a terrine with salt pork, line bottom and sides of terrine with the rectangles, leaving a ½ inch overhang on sides and 1 inch at ends. Fold up overhang, then arrange inch wide strips of salt pork in a crosshatch pattern over the top. Tuck in at the edges. If using this method, cover the terrine with foil for the first 1½ hours of cooking to prevent strips from curling up and becoming too cooked.

Salt pork open

To line a terrine with bacon, blanch bacon 5 minutes and dry on paper toweling. Arrange strips neatly overlapping in a lengthwise pattern, cutting where necessary to fit the shape of the terrine. As with fatback, allow a 1½ inch overhang on the ends and a ½ inch overhang on sides.

It used to be customary to cool and age pâtés under a weight to push fat out and make the loaf more dense. Now, we usually skip this step: fat has already been reduced in these recipes, and we find weighting makes the meat tougher in many cases. One exception is the *terrine de poissons*, which is weighted overnight to push out water as it cools and sets up. **Weighting a terrine** requires having on hand a board, plate, or large can which just fits inside the rim of the terrine. If using a board or plate, place a small can or some other weight on top of it.

Country style terrines, such as *pâté maison*, are traditionally presented in an oval ceramic or glazed pottery terrine. However, a simple aluminum loaf pan from the grocery store will serve well enough for the cooking, and then the pâté can be unmolded before serving. To **unmold a terrine,** immerse the mold in 2 inches of hot water, or run a trickle of hot water over the bottom and sides to loosen. If pâté does not come right out when the terrine is inverted, insert a knife between mold and pâté to loosen. If it still does not slip out, repeat the hot water treatment briefly. When the pâté is out of the terrine, wipe off any excess fat. Aspic collected on the outside of the pâte is quite tasty. It may be separated from the excess fat and served with the pâté.

Pâtés that are not glazed with aspic or wrapped in pastry crust may be **sealed** under a layer of fat to preserve longer. To seal, refrigerate pâté, still in its cooking terrine, overnight. Next day, heat just to the melting point 1½ cups fat—lard, poultry fat, or clarified butter, whichever taste is best. Pour over the pâté in the terrine and chill to set the fat. The pâté will keep wrapped and refrigerated for 10 days to 3 weeks. Scoop fat away before serving or unmolding.

Terrines, pâtés, and galantines lend themselves to a huge variety of serving presentations from the homeliest and most casual to the very fancy. Suggestions for accompanying condiments and forms of presentation in the following recipes are one vision. There is always room for the cook's own imagination.

PÂTÉ MAISON

Our house pâté is a basic country style terrine for those who like the taste of liver. A simple forcemeat of pork and pork liver is seasoned with thyme, garlic, shallot, and white wine and baked in a wrapping of caul fat. Quick and easy to make, pâté maison is ideal picnic or lunch food. Pork liver, which is delicious and nutritious, is available in Oriental and Italian markets, as well as many supermarkets. Beef liver can be substituted, but the flavor is not as subtle.

--------------------- For a 3½ pound terrine ---------------------

For grinding, medium plate:
> 2½ pounds pork butt
> 1½ pounds pork liver
> ½ pound fatback
> 2 shallots, peeled
> 2 garlic cloves, peeled

For seasoning:
> 1 teaspoon fresh thyme leaves, or ¼ teaspoon dried
> 1 teaspoon chopped fresh sage leaves, or ¼ teaspoon dried
> 2 teaspoons salt
> 1 teaspoon black pepper
> 2 eggs
> ⅓ cup white wine
>
> 1 sheet caul fat, for lining the terrine
> 1 bay leaf

Grind together meats, fat, shallots, and garlic. Or with a chef's knife, chop meats and fat fine and mince garlic and shallots. Add seasonings and mix until well blended. If using an electric mixer rather than hands, do not overmix or meat will become tough.

Preheat oven to 325 degrees. Line a 2 quart terrine or loaf pan with caul. Fill with forcemeat, top with the bay leaf, and enclose with caul, trimming off excess and tucking in ends. Pat surface with palm, then rap terrine on the counter to jar out air pockets.

To cook, bake in a *bain-marie* 2 hours, or until an instant reading meat thermometer registers 200 degrees and juices are golden with no trace of pink remaining. Remove and cool to room temperature. To allow flavors to blend, refrigerate at least overnight. Will keep wrapped and refrigerated up to 10 days, or up to 3 weeks sealed under fat, wrapped, and refrigerated.

To serve, unmold or leave in the terrine and cut into ⅛ inch thick slices. Accompany with Dijon mustard, *cornichons,* and French bread.

Sage

PÂTÉ CAMPAGNE

Pâté campagne *is a close cousin of* pâté maison. *Veal replaces the pork liver and sage is added to the forcemeat to produce a hearty, herbaceous country pâté for those who do not like the taste of liver. The procedure and uses are similar to those of* pâté maison, *and the ingredients are readily available in American markets. The forcemeat is refrigerated overnight before cooking to improve the flavor, texture, and color of this terrine which will be blander, less firm, and grayish if the step is skipped.*

──────────────── For a 3½ pound terrine ────────────────

For grinding, medium plate:

  2½ pounds pork butt
  ¾ pound veal
  ¼ pound ham
  ¾ pound fatback
  3 shallots, peeled
  2 garlic cloves, peeled

For the seasoning:

  1½ teaspoons fresh thyme leaves, or ½ teaspoon dried
  2 teaspoons salt
  1 teaspoon black pepper
  1 egg
  ½ cup white wine

  1 sheet caul fat, for lining the terrine
  1 bay leaf

Grind together meats, fat, shallots, and garlic. Or with a chef's knife, chop meats and fat fine and mince shallots and garlic. Add seasonings and mix until well blended. If using an electric mixer rather than hands, do not overmix or meat will become tough.

Line a 2 quart terrine or loaf pan with caul. Fill with forcemeat, packing down as you go to avoid air pockets. Place bay leaf on top, and enclose with caul, trimming off excess and tucking in ends. Refrigerate overnight. Remove from refrigerator 1 hour before cooking.

To cook, preheat oven to 325 degrees. Bake in a *bain-marie* 1¾ hours, or until an instant reading meat thermometer registers 165 degrees. Remove from oven and allow to cool to room temperature. To allow flavors to blend, refrigerate at least overnight. Will keep wrapped and refrigerated up to 10 days, or up to 3 weeks sealed under fat, wrapped, and refrigerated.

To serve, unmold or leave in the terrine and cut into ⅛ inch thick slices. Accompany with Dijon mustard, *cornichons*, and French bread.

Thyme

DUTCH MOTHER TERRINE

This is an adaptation of a recipe given to us by Mr. Alfred Peet, master coffee roaster and founder of Peet's Coffees and Teas. When we opened Pig-by-the-Tail, he was so delighted to have a European style delicatessen in the neighborhood that he offered us his mother's pâté recipe for our repertoire. We were intrigued by the unusual combination of beef liver with tarragon and a soupçon of vinegar. He agreed we made a very tasty version, although we could never get ours to taste like his mother's. Dutch mother terrine is best cooked in a ceramic terrine suitable for table service because the encasing aspic is difficult to unmold. If canned beef bouillon is used for the stock, dilute with 1½ parts water to 1 part bouillon to reduce the saltiness and soften the flavor. If using beef bouillon cubes, dissolve 2 cubes in 1 cup water.

──────────────── For a 3½ pound terrine ────────────────

For grinding, medium plate:
> 1 pound beef liver
> 1 pound veal
> 1 pound pork butt
> ¼ pound fatback
> 2 shallots

For seasoning:
> 1 tablespoon fresh tarragon leaves, or 1 teaspoon dried
> 1½ teaspoons salt
> 1 teaspoon black pepper
> 1 egg
> ½ cup red wine
> 1 tablespoon red wine vinegar

> 1 sheet caul fat, for lining the terrine
> 1 bay leaf

For the aspic:

1 teaspoon unflavored gelatin
1 cup rich beef stock

Grind together beef liver, veal, pork, fatback, and shallots. Or mince with a chef's knife. Add seasoning ingredients and mix thoroughly.

Preheat oven to 450 degrees. Line a 2 quart terrine or loaf pan with caul. Fill with forcemeat, place bay leaf on top, and enclose with caul, trimming off excess and tucking in ends. Place directly in the oven and cook 10 minutes.

Dissolve gelatin in beef stock and pour into the terrine. Reduce oven heat to 350 degrees and continue cooking 1 hour and 50 minutes, or until an instant reading meat thermometer registers 190 degrees. Remove, cool to room temperature, and refrigerate overnight. Will keep wrapped and refrigerated up to 5 days.

To serve, present in its terrine and cut into $3/16$ inch thick slices, making sure to dish out some of the aspic with each portion. Accompany with a bowl of pickled onions and warm French bread.

PICKLED ONIONS:

Peel 2 pounds red or white onions and slice into thin rounds. Place in a bowl and set aside. In a small nonreactive saucepan, mix together 1 cup red wine vinegar, $1/3$ cup water, and 1 tablespoon sugar. Bring to a boil, then pour over onions. Let cool, then chill several hours. Will keep stored in the liquid and refrigerated up to 2 weeks.

PÂTÉ RIS DE VEAU

Pâté ris de veau *is a simple country terrine dressed up for a party by adding a layer of sweetbreads and carrots in the center so that a colorful mosaic is exposed when the pâté is sliced. Veal sweetbreads are most delicate, but beef will do, or follow Jane Grigson's suggestion and use lamb sweetbreads if you can find them. As with pâté campagne, flavors blend and color is enhanced if the terrine is refrigerated overnight before cooking.*

――――――――――― For a 3½ pound terrine ―――――――――――

³/₄ pound beef or veal sweetbreads
2 medium size carrots

For grinding, medium plate:

1½ pounds pork butt
³/₄ pound veal
¼ pound mild ham
¼ pound fatback
2 shallots, peeled
2 garlic cloves, peeled

For seasoning:

2 teaspoons fresh thyme leaves, or ½ teaspoon dried
1 teaspoon pâté spice (see page 5)
½ teaspoon white pepper
2 teaspoons salt
1 egg
²/₃ cup heavy cream

³/₄ to ⁷/₈ pound fatback, cut for lining a terrine

To prepare sweetbreads, place in a medium size pot, cover with water by 4 inches, and bring to a boil. Simmer over medium heat 1 hour. Drain in a colander, and cool enough to handle. With fingers, remove outer membrane and connecting filament from underside, and discard. Slice sweetbreads ¼ inch thick and set aside.

To prepare carrots, peel and cut at 45 degree angle into ⅛ inch thick slices. Set aside.

Grind together pork, veal, ham, fatback, shallots, and garlic. Or chop fine with a knife. Add seasoning ingredients to meats and mix until well blended.

Line a 2 quart terrine or loaf pan with fatback and pack half the forcemeat in the bottom. Pat down, then make a well in the center to within 1 inch of the sides. Place sliced sweetbreads down the center, then top with carrots arranged flat side down and slightly overlapping to cover the surface of sweetbreads. Fill terrine with remaining forcemeat. Cover with fatback slices and enclose neatly. Pat down to eliminate air pockets. Cover with foil and pinch around edges to seal. Refrigerate overnight. Remove from refrigerator 1 hour before cooking.

To cook, preheat oven to 350 degrees. Bake the terrine in a *bain-marie* 2 hours, or until an instant reading meat thermometer registers 175 degrees. Remove from oven and serve warm, or cool to room temperature and refrigerate overnight. Will keep wrapped and refrigerated up to 1 week or up to 2 weeks sealed under fat.

To serve, unmold or leave in the terrine and cut into ⅜ inch thick slices. Arrange on a serving platter or individual plates and garnish with *cornichons* and Niçoise olives. Accompany with warm French bread and a pot of Dijon mustard.

TERRINE DE LAPIN MON ONCLE

When our friend Mijo's uncle was visiting from Lyons one summer, he kindly gave us his recipe for rabbit terrine, the best we've tried. The procedure has many steps, but once the rabbit is boned this recipe is actually easier than some others for the home cook. Rabbit is generally available in butcher shops and supermarkets, and no special equipment is required as the rabbit meat is hand cut. Grinding or food processing rabbit, which is nonfatty and nongelatinous, would ruin the texture and eliminate the pleasing contrast between julienned strips of meat and ground sausage in the pâté.

―――――――――― For a 2½ pound terrine ――――――――――

1 large rabbit, 3½ to 4 pounds

For the stock:

>**the rabbit bones**
>**1 small bay leaf**
>**2 juniper berries**
>**1 cup white wine**
>**3 cups water**

>**2 ounces French bread, about a 3 inch piece of baguette**
>**1 egg**
>**¼ cup brandy**
>**1 chicken liver**
>**¾ pound Toulouse sausage meat (see page 78), not in casing**

For seasoning:

>**2 teaspoons fresh thyme leaves, or ½ teaspoon dried**
>**½ teaspoon fennel seed**
>**½ teaspoon pâté spice (see page 5)**
>**¼ teaspoon white pepper**

1 teaspoon salt
½ cup rabbit stock

1 bay leaf
¾ pound bacon, blanched 5 minutes, for lining the
    terrine

To prepare rabbit (see illustrations on page 28), pull out kidneys and liver from cavity and set aside. Use a curved boning knife to remove meat from legs and thighs. Set aside with kidneys and livers. Sever leg/ thigh bones at back and place in a medium size pot. Next, sever front leg joints at shoulder on both sides. Remove meat from front legs, set aside with the rest of the meat and add bones to the pot. Insert the boning knife into meat right next to bone at top of back and cut down back and out along ribs on both sides. Add meat to meat pile. Remove small fillets next to the bone on underside of rabbit and add to meat pile. Break carcass in half and add to pot. You should wind up with a pot of bones and a pile of meat, kidneys, and liver.

To make stock, add bay leaf, juniper berries, wine and water to bones, set over medium heat, and simmer 1 hour. Strain into bowl and set aside to cool. Discard bones.

To make forcemeat, cut up French bread and place, along with egg and brandy, in a bowl large enough to hold meats. With a chef's knife, cut rabbit into ⅜ inch wide strips—doesn't matter how long—and add to bowl. Roughly chop kidneys, liver, and chicken liver and add to bowl. Add sausage, seasoning ingredients, and ½ cup of the strained rabbit stock. Mix well with hands, breaking up sausage and bread. Set aside.

Preheat oven to 350 degrees. To assemble, line a 2 quart terrine or loaf pan with blanched bacon strips. Pack forcemeat into terrine, top with bay leaf, and cover with remaining bacon, enclosing neatly. Cover with lid or foil.

To cook, bake in a *bain-marie* 1 hour, then remove lid or foil. Continue cooking 30 to 45 minutes, or until an instant reading meat thermometer registers 165 degrees. Remove from oven and cool to room temperature. To allow flavors to blend, refrigerate at least overnight, up to 2 days. Will keep wrapped and refrigerated 5 or 6 days, but will dry out after that.

To serve, unmold or leave in the terrine and cut into ¼ inch thick slices. Accompany with Dijon mustard, *cornichons*, and dense brown bread.

Start cut at top of neck

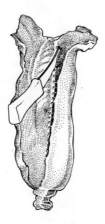

Cut around ribs

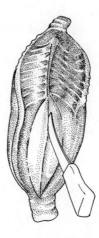

Cut out fillets

PÂTÉ DE POULET

Pâté de poulet *was discovered by a felicitous mistake when we first opened the shop. We had made much too much* boudin blanc *stuffing: how to avoid throwing it away? We filled a terrine, adding sorrel in the center for color relief, and* voilà, *a dish that has become a long time favorite. This pâté is an exception to our normal style of reducing fat in traditional recipes; here, a larger proportion is required to retain succulence in the final product. The tart taste of sorrel in the center makes the pâté very special, but sorrel is hard to find in markets. You can substitute fresh spinach tossed with the juice of half a lemon.*

--------------------------- For a 3²/₃ pound pâté ---------------------------

For the center:

      1 pound fresh sorrel, 2 to 3 bunches depending on season and size of bunches

For grinding, fine plate:

      2 ounces French bread, about a 3 inch piece of baguette
      ¹/₂ cup half and half
      1 pound pork butt
      1 pound chicken breast, boned but not skinned
      ³/₄ pound fatback
      ¹/₂ pound yellow onions, peeled

For seasoning:

      ¹/₄ teaspoon grated nutmeg
      1 teaspoon pâté spice (see page 5)
      1 teaspoon white pepper
      2 teaspoons salt
      1 egg

      ³/₄ to ⁷/₈ pound fatback, cut for lining a terrine

To prepare sorrel, bring 3 quarts water to a boil. Choose 2 perfect leaves and set aside for final garnish. Cut remaining leaves crosswise into ¼ inch thick strips and chop up stems. Immerse in boiling water and immediately drain in a colander. Set aside.

Cube French bread and soak in half and half 15 minutes to soften. Squeeze out and reserve half and half.

To prepare forcemeat, grind meats, fat, onions, and soaked French bread. Be sure to save out ¼ pound fatback to push last ingredients through. Add half and half and seasoning ingredients. Beat with an electric mixer, starting on low speed and working up to high speed, until light and fluffy, about 3 minutes.

If using a food processor, remove skins from chicken breasts and substitute an equal amount of fatback. Purée together all ingredients for grinding, including half and half, in several batches. Beat in seasoning ingredients with an electric mixer or heavy wire whip.

Preheat oven to 325 degrees. To assemble, line a 2 quart terrine or loaf pan with fatback. Place half the forcemeat on the bottom and push into corners to fill all spaces. Make a small well about 3 inches wide down the center, pushing some forcemeat toward edges. Fill well with sorrel, then fill terrine with remaining forcemeat. Pat top vigorously with palm of hand, then rap terrine on counter to eliminate air pockets. Cover with fatback, folding edges neatly over center pieces, then with foil, pinching around edges to seal. Prick foil in 2 places to allow steam to escape.

To cook, bake in a *bain-marie* 1¾ hours, or until an instant reading meat thermometer registers 162 degrees. Remove from oven, cool to room temperature, and refrigerate overnight, up to 2 days. Will keep wrapped and refrigerated up to 1 week, or up to 2 weeks sealed under fat.

To serve, unmold and with fingers carefully remove excess rendered fat from outside, taking care not to disturb symmetry of fatback covering. Press reserved sorrel leaves onto top. Cut pâté into ⅛ inch thick slices and accompany with dense brown bread and a pot of Dijon mustard.

PÂTÉ PUR FOIE TRUFFÉ

Serve pâté pur foie truffé as a first course before a winter holiday dinner when the black truffles are fresh and spirits run high. If the truffle extravagance called for in this recipe is out of the question, substitute an equal amount of chopped, toasted pistachio nuts. The Madeira adds a whiff of sweetness especially suitable in combination with pork liver and truffle.

──────────── For a 4 pound pâté ────────────

3 pounds pork liver
1/2 pound sweet butter
1 1/2 pounds fatback
1 teaspoon fresh chopped sage leaves, or 1/2 teaspoon
    dried
1 teaspoon fresh thyme leaves, or 1/2 teaspoon dried
1/2 teaspoon fresh chopped rosemary, or 1/4 teaspoon
    dried
1 1/2 teaspoons salt
1 teaspoon black pepper
2 eggs
2 to 3 ounces fresh black truffle, roughly chopped
2 tablespoons dry Madeira wine

3/4 to 7/8 pound fatback, cut for lining a terrine

Trim off gristle and cut pork liver into 2 inch wide strips. In a sauté pan, melt butter until foaming. Add liver and cook over medium heat 15 to 20 minutes, until firm but still pink in center. Remove pan from heat and let liver cool 15 minutes. If using a food processor instead of a grinder, cut liver into 1/2 inch dice and sauté 8 minutes.

Using the medium plate, grind together liver and fatback, pouring through juices accumulated in the sauté pan as you grind. Or, using a food processor, puree liver and fat in several batches, adding accumulated pan juices while processing. Pull out and discard any uncut gristle. Add seasoning ingredients and mix until thoroughly blended.

Preheat oven to 350 degrees. Line a 2 quart terrine or loaf pan with fatback and fill with pâté mixture. Cover with fatback, folding edges neatly over center pieces. Cook in a *bain-marie* 1½ hours, or until an instant reading meat thermometer registers 180 degrees. Fatback on top will be quite browned and curled up; it is removed before serving. Remove pâté from oven and cool to room temperature. To allow flavors to blend, cover and refrigerate at least overnight, up to 2 days. Will keep wrapped and refrigerated up to 1 week or up to 3 weeks sealed under fat.

To serve, peel fatback off top, then unmold. Slice ⅜ inch thick and arrange on a plate or platter and garnish with thin slices of papaya. Accompany with French bread and a full bodied white Burgundy or good Sauternes.

DUCK LIVER MOUSSE

The beginning of my love for charcuterie and its wonderful concoctions can be traced directly to the first such dish I ever tasted, Michael Field's chicken liver pâté. Years later, we replaced chicken livers with the more exotic, slightly sweeter duck livers, incorporated herbs, and added a glistening gelée cap for eye appeal in the deli case. Variations aside, the idea remains the same, and the dish is just as good made with chicken livers if you don't have an Oriental market where you can buy duck livers. Chicken livers are a little drier and will require a bit more cream. For a simple presentation, we suggest packing the mousse into a crock and covering with rendered duck fat or clarified butter to seal out air. Instructions for a fancier presentation in an aspic covered mold are given at the end of the recipe.

——————— Hors d'oeuvre for 6 or a buffet dish for 10 ———————

3 tablespoons butter
1 pound duck or chicken livers
$1/2$ teaspoon chopped fresh sage leaves, or $1/4$ teaspoon
    dried
$1/4$ teaspoon white pepper
$1/4$ cup brandy

3 tablespoons butter
1 small onion, peeled and roughly chopped
1 small tart apple, unpeeled, cored, and roughly
    chopped
1 teaspoon fresh thyme leaves, or $1/2$ teaspoon dried

$1/4$ pound butter, at room temperature
5 tablespoons heavy cream

1 ounce blanched almonds
2 tablespoons butter

4 tablespoons clarified butter or rendered duck fat

In a sauté pan, melt 3 tablespoons butter until foaming, then add livers, sage, and white pepper. Cook 10 to 12 minutes until livers are firm but still pink in centers. Raise heat, add brandy, and ignite with a match. Shake pan vigorously for a minute until alcohol burns off and flame dies. Remove livers to a large bowl where juices can collect.

In the same pan, melt 3 more tablespoons butter and add onion, apple, and thyme. Cook over medium low heat 20 to 25 minutes until apple and onion are cooked through. Remove to bowl with livers. Allow to cool to room temperature.

To make the mousse, use a food processor or electric blender to purée livers, apple, and onion until quite smooth, along with any collected juices, butter, and cream. Or, using the small plate, grind together livers, apple, and onion along with any collected juices twice, pushing butter through after second time. Disassemble grinder to retrieve butter caught inside, then whip in the cream with an electric mixer. Set mousse aside.

To prepare almonds, pulverize them, without completely puréeing, in a blender or food processor. Melt 2 tablespoons butter in a sauté pan, add nuts, and stir constantly over medium heat until browned and the nutty smell emerges. Remove to paper toweling and set aside.

To finish, pack mousse into a 3 cup crock using a wooden spoon. Press down and smooth out as you go. Spread toasted nuts over top and pour clarified butter or rendered duck fat over all. Cover with plastic wrap after fat is set. Refrigerate 3 hours or overnight. Will keep refrigerated up to 10 days sealed under fat.

To serve, remove from refrigerator 30 minutes before using. Spread on water biscuits or matzoh crackers and accompany with a full bodied white or rosé wine.

For a fancier presentation, pour ½ cup melted aspic into a 2 cup mold and refrigerate until set. Spread toasted nuts over the aspic, then pack mousse into the mold. Chill 4 hours or overnight. To serve, run hot water over outside of mold for 20 seconds, insert knife blade between mousse and mold to loosen, then invert onto plate. Mousse should come right out. If it doesn't, run a little more hot water over outside. Mousse will keep in this form up to 5 days.

For the aspic:

½ cup clear chicken stock
1 tablespoon sherry
1 teaspoon unflavored gelatin

In a small saucepan bring chicken stock to a boil. In a small bowl, dissolve gelatin in the sherry, whisk into the boiling stock, and immediately remove from heat. Aspic will be rubbery if allowed to boil. Pour through a strainer lined with a clean cloth into a clean bowl.

PÂTÉ DE JAMBON EN CROÛTE

Pâté wrapped in pastry crust makes a light luncheon or picnic meal with no further ado save for an accompanying green vegetable such as asparagus, green beans, or Belgian endive. The mustard cream sauce suggested here will be suitable for both the pâté and the vegetable. A fancy hinged mold may be used to form pâté en croûte, but it is not necessary. We describe a handy technique for the home cook, learned from Madame DesChamps while apprenticing in her Le Vivoir Restaurant in Sausalito: the forcemeat is rolled in the pastry and cooked on a baking sheet with no mold at all. Decorated with pastry cutouts, the result is just as pretty and the danger of soggy crust on the sides is avoided.

For a 3 pound pâté

For the pastry crust:

> 1½ cups all purpose white flour
> ⅛ teaspoon salt
> 6 tablespoons butter or rendered pork fat, at room temperature
> 1 egg yolk plus enough cold water to make ⅓ cup

For grinding, small plate:

> 1½ pounds mild ham
> 1 pound pork butt
> 2 shallots, peeled
> 1 large garlic clove, peeled

For seasoning:

> 2 teaspoons fresh tarragon leaves, or ½ teaspoon dried
> 4 tablespoons chopped fresh parsley
> ⅓ teaspoon cayenne
> 1 egg
> ¾ cup heavy cream

10 inch square caul fat

For glazing the crust:
    1 egg yolk
    2 teaspoons half and half or milk

To make the pastry, measure flour and salt into a medium size bowl. Cut butter into bits and work into flour using fingers or 2 forks until mixture consists of little balls. Mix egg yolk and water together, then add to flour and butter. Gather dough into a ball, wrap in plastic, and smooth out between thumbs and fingers. Refrigerate 2 hours, up to 2 days. Remove from refrigerator 1 hour before using.

To make forcemeat, grind meats, shallots, and garlic. Or mince in a food processor without puréeing. Mix in seasoning ingredients and blend well. Set aside.

To assemble pâté, roll out pastry on a floured surface into a 14 inch by 16 inch rectangle ⅛ inch thick. Form forcemeat into a long cylinder 4 inches in diameter, patting with hands and rolling to eliminate air pockets. Wrap caul fat around forcemeat and place on pastry parallel to the longer edge. Roll up pastry to enclose, as tightly as possible without tearing, and brush edge with water to seal. Trim excess pastry off ends and set aside for decorating. Neatly fold end flaps together and seal with water. Dust entire surface with flour. Roll out trimmings and cut into decorative shapes. Set aside. Mix egg yolk with half and half or milk to make egg glaze and brush onto pastry. Arrange cutouts on top, pressing down lightly to seal, and brush cutouts with more of the egg glaze.

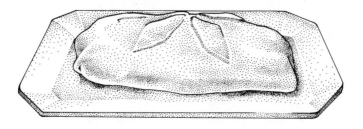

Pâté de jambon en croûte

Pâté may be cooked immediately or wrapped in plastic and refrigerated overnight if it is to be served warm the next day. In this case, chill uncovered until glaze is set. If you wrap it before glaze is set, plastic wrap will stick and make a mess. Remove from refrigerator 1 hour before cooking.

To cook, preheat oven to 425 degrees. Place pâté on a baking sheet in the oven. After 10 minutes, reduce heat to 350 degrees and continue cooking 45 minutes. Raise oven heat to 425 degrees and cook 15 minutes more, until crust is quite golden and an instant reading meat thermometer registers 180 degrees. Remove and serve warm, or let cool to room temperature and refrigerate overnight, up to 2 days.

To serve, slice ½ inch thick and accompany with a mustard cream sauce made by mixing together ¼ cup Dijon mustard with ¾ cup heavy cream and 1½ teaspoons chopped fresh tarragon leaves or ½ teaspoon dried.

GALANTINE OF CHICKEN

If the idea of making a galantine seems like contemplating im-
ponderables, galantine of chicken is a good place to start. A
chicken is not hard to bone, and the result is visually satisfying
even when the job is not so neatly done. Galantine of chicken
is a versatile dish. Serve it cold as an hors d'oeuvre or picnic
food, or warm as a main dish, in which case it may properly be
called a ballottine. As an added boon, the stock in which the
galantine is poached can be turned into a delicious light soup.
Just cook a little pasta in it and garnish with green onion slivers.

Dinner for 4, hors d'oeuvre for 6,
or a buffet platter for 10

3½ pound frying chicken
1 teaspoon fresh thyme leaves, or ½ teaspoon dried
½ teaspoon coriander seed, cracked
½ teaspoon salt

For the poaching stock:
the giblets and bones from the chicken
1 carrot, cut in 1 inch pieces
1 small onion, unpeeled and quartered
1 bay leaf
1 cup beef bouillon
6 cups water

2 large leaves fresh chard

For the ham mousse stuffing:
¼ pound mild ham
1 large shallot, peeled
1 teaspoon chopped fresh tarragon leaves, or ¼ teaspoon dried
¼ teaspoon black pepper
¼ cup heavy cream

For browning the galantine:

    2 tablespoons butter
    1 tablespoon olive or peanut oil

To prepare chicken, remove neck and giblets and set aside. With a boning knife, sever wings at elbow joints and set aside with neck and giblets. Make a circular cut through skin and flesh 1 inch up from bottom of each leg. Place chicken breast side down and cut through skin

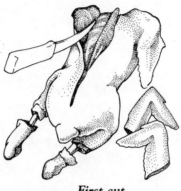

First cut

and flesh down length of back. Working from backbone out and around ribs, remove meat from bones, leaving skin attached to meat. Sever thigh

Bone around ribs

joints at backbone when you get there. Sever wings at shoulder joints and continue around to breastbone. Remove carcass and set aside with giblet pile. Insert knife into flesh next to thigh bone and work knife

Sever thigh joint

around thigh bone to free the bone. Sever thigh bone at leg joint and add bone to giblet pile. Insert knife into flesh next to leg bone, free flesh from leg bone down to circular cut at bottom. Pull out leg bone and add to giblet pile. Remove thigh and leg bones from other side and both wing

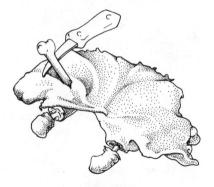

Leg joint cut free

bones in the same way. Add bones to giblet pile. Don't worry if some meat falls free while boning. You should wind up with a boneless chicken, perhaps some pieces of meat, and a pile of neck, giblets, wing tips, carcass, thigh, leg, and wing bones.

To prepare poaching stock, put all stock ingredients plus everything from giblet and bone pile into a large pot. Add more water if liquid does not cover bones. Bring to a boil, reduce heat, and simmer 1½ hours. Pour through a strainer lined with clean cloth into a clean pot. Set aside.

Wilt chard leaves by dropping them into hot stock for 30 seconds. Remove, pat dry, and set aside.

To prepare stuffing, swirl ingredients in a food processor or blender. Or grind ham and shallot using the small plate, then whip in tarragon, black pepper, and cream with an electric mixer. Or use a chef's knife to mince ham and shallot, then beat in remaining ingredients with an electric mixer. Set aside.

To assemble galantine, place chicken skin side down and patch any bare spots with any spare pieces of meat. Sprinkle with thyme, coriander, and salt. Spread chard over entire surface. Roll ham mousse into a cylinder the same length as the chicken from neck to tail. Place the ham mousse cylinder lengthwise in the center of chard leaves. Fold one side of chicken up over ham mousse, then continue rolling up. Tuck in ends. Place chicken roll on a 12 inch square of cheesecloth and roll up to encase chicken. Tie off ends of cheesecloth with string, then tie string around chicken roll at 2 inch intervals to secure.

*Chicken galantine,
rolled and tied*

To cook, bring poaching stock to a boil. Heat butter and oil in a sauté pan until foaming, then sauté chicken roll wrapped in cheesecloth 10 minutes, turning to brown all around. Drop into poaching liquid, reduce heat, and simmer 30 minutes, turning from time to time. Remove pot from heat and let sit 20 minutes. Remove galantine and let it rest 10 minutes. Serve warm, or cool to room temperature and refrigerate overnight still wrapped in cheesecloth. Reserve poaching liquid for another use. Galantine will keep wrapped and refrigerated up to 1 week.

To serve, cut strings and unroll cheesecloth. If serving hot, slice ¼ inch thick and accompany with a puree of potato and celery root. If serving cold, slice ⅛ inch thick, arrange slices on a platter or individual plates, and garnish with a spoonful of **celery root** *rémoulade* (see page 193).

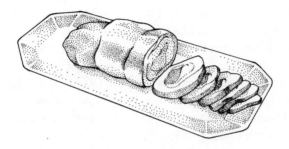

Galantine cooked and cut

GALANTINE OF TURKEY

Our turkey galantine is a result of my brief apprenticeship at the charcuterie of M. Roger Gleize in Revel, 60 kilometers west of Toulouse, where I had gone to learn the secrets of ham curing and Toulouse sausage. In addition to these regional specialties for which Monsieur Gleize enjoys a wide reputation, he also manufactures a wonderful tinned turkey galantine which he ships all over France. I was intrigued to discover turkey charcuterie in a remote village of southwestern France, and it was the first dish I made when I got home, throwing in a bit more of my newly acquired knowledge in the form of Toulouse sausage and adding green peppercorns for flair. The green peppercorns work well here, but if you can't find them, cracked black pepper may be substituted. Making turkey galantine is very similar to the procedure described for chicken galantine except that the skin, which fits loosely on this bird, is removed before the meat is taken off the bones.

---------------- For a buffet or picnic dish for 35 to 40 ----------------

10 to 12 pound hen turkey

For the stock:

> **the giblets, wing tips, and bones from the turkey**
> **1 carrot, unpeeled and cut into 1 inch pieces**
> **1 onion, unpeeled and quartered**
> **3 sprigs fresh thyme, or 1 pinch dried**
> **1 bay leaf**
> **12 cups water**

For the forcemeat:

> **1/2 pound salt pork or ham fat**
> **1/3 baguette or 3 ounces French bread**

1 cup brandy

3 eggs

2 pounds Toulouse sausage (see page 78), not in casing

3½ ounce can green peppercorns, drained

1 tablespoon fresh thyme leaves, or 1 teaspoon dried

2 teaspoons pâté spice (see page 5)

1 tablespoon salt

To prepare turkey, remove neck and giblets and set aside. Using a curved boning knife, sever wings at elbow joints and set aside with giblets. Cut off tail and set aside with giblets.

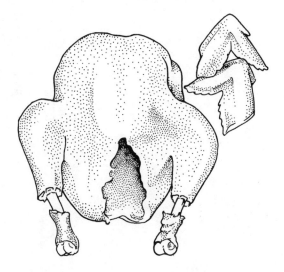

Turkey on back, wing tips on side

Next, remove turkey skin. Cut through skin in a circle 2 inches up from the bottom of each leg. Place turkey breast side down and cut through skin and meat down length of backbone. Starting at top of backbone, lift skin up with thumb and forefinger and carefully cut skin away from meat. Continue pulling and cutting skin away from meat down length of backbone and then out and around to breast on each side. The hard part is under wings, under thighs, and at the neckline where skin is firmly attached to meat. However, tears in skin can be

Terrines, Pâtés & Galantines

Work skin free

repaired later. When you get to the breast and legs, loosen skin from meat with hands, then pull skin down each leg to free. Set skin aside.

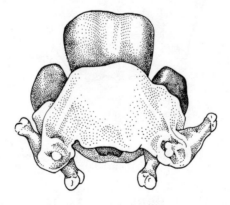

Pull skin towards legs

Still using the curved boning knife, sever legs at thigh joints to free legs. Set aside for another dish: turkey legs are too full of splinters to bone and are better put to another use. Remove meat from bones in the same manner described in the **chicken galantine** recipe (see pages 40–41).

Add bones to giblet pile. You should now have a pile of giblets, wing tips, and bones; a turkey skin; a pile of turkey meat; and two legs for another dish.

To prepare stock, place everything from giblet pile plus stock ingredients in a large pot. Break up carcass if too large for the pot, and add more water if liquid does not cover bones. Bring to a boil, reduce heat, and simmer 1½ hours. Pour through a strainer lined with clean cloth into a bowl and set aside.

If using salt pork, remove rind and set aside for another purpose. Rinse salt pork, then blanch in boiling water 15 minutes. Drain and pat dry. When cool enough to handle, grind, using small plate, or mince with a chef's knife. If using ham fat, grind or mince.

To prepare forcemeat, cube bread and place in a large bowl with brandy and eggs. Cut turkey breasts into ¼ inch wide strips. Roughly chop remaining turkey meat. Add all the turkey meat to bowl, along with salt pork or ham fat, sausage, seasonings, and 1½ cups stock. Reserve remaining stock for another dish. Mix with hands, crumbling bread and breaking up sausage to distribute evenly throughout mixture.

To assemble the galantine, lay turkey skin out flat with breast side down. With string or heavy thread, tie off wing and leg ends. With

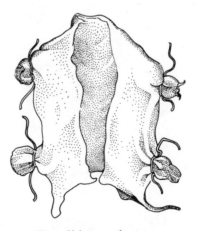

Tie off legs and wings

needle and thread, repair rips in skin. Pack some forcemeat into wing and leg cavities, then mound the rest in a loaf shape in the center of the skin, patting all over to remove air pockets. Pull skin over stuffing

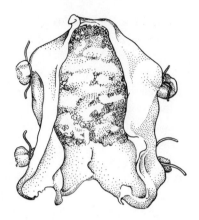

Fill from front opening

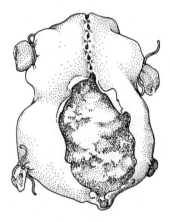

Sew shut

to enclose, and stitch together with needle and thread. The galantine will look a little flat at this point. There are two ways to plump it up. The first is to tie with string. First tie crosswise around each end somewhat loosely, then tie crosswise around middle in two places. Place seam side down in roasting pan. Or, to produce a more turkeylike form, place galantine seam side down in a roasting pan just large enough to fit it.

Tuck potatoes or onions between legs and at sides to prop the galantine into a turkey shape.

Place in pan to cook

To cook, preheat oven to 350 degrees. Bake galantine 2 hours, or until an instant reading meat thermometer registers 165 degrees. Remove from oven, cool to room temperature, cover, and refrigerate overnight.

To serve, present on a platter and accompany with warm French bread and a bowl of **pickled cherries** (see page 261). Cut into ¼ inch thick slices, then cut each slice in half. Galantine will keep moist up to 5 days if wrapped and refrigerated.

The Turkey Legs:

Add some peeled and slivered garlic, an onion peeled and cut up, and a few herbs such as thyme and bay to turkey stock. Season with salt and pepper to taste and poach turkey legs in stock for 25 minutes. Remove legs and set aside. Strain broth into a clean pot. Add 2 stalks of celery and 2 carrots, cut up as you like. Cook until vegetables are *al dente,* then add ½ cup cooked rice and the turkey legs. Heat through. Stir in 1 tablespoon soy sauce and 1 tablespoon lemon juice, dish up into 2 big bowls, and sprinkle a handful of chopped fresh herbs over the top of each bowl.

GALANTINE OF DUCK

Galantine of duck is for a special occasion. Presented under a glistening coat of aspic on a shimmering bed of cubed aspic, the galantine is lovely to look at. It also involves an elaborate procedure starting one day and finishing two days later. If at all possible, use fresh duck—Long Island or Peking style white Pekins or Muscovies—for this recipe. The dried mushrooms and bouillon cube in the stock are for coloring.

_____ For a 4½ pound galantine, hors d'oeuvre _____
for 20, or a buffet platter for 30

2 ducks, 4½ to 5 pounds each

For marinating:

> **the duck breasts, hearts, livers, and meat**
> **¼ cup red wine**
> **freshly ground black pepper**

For the stock:

> **the duck necks, gizzards, wing tips, carcasses, and bones**
> **2 sprigs fresh thyme**
> **1 bay leaf**
> **1 small onion, unpeeled and roughly chopped**
> **1 carrot, unpeeled and roughly chopped**
> **2 dried shiitake or porcini (cepes) mushrooms**
> **1 beef bouillon cube**
> **6 cups water**

For grinding, small plate:

> **the marinated duck meat, minus the breasts, hearts, and**
>   **livers**
> **1½ pounds pork butt**
> **¼ pound mild ham**
> **1 medium onion**

For seasoning the forcemeat:

>the grated peel of ½ an orange
>2 teaspoons fresh thyme leaves, or ½ teaspoon dried
>2½ teaspoons salt
>1 teaspoon black pepper
>2 eggs
>⅓ cup brandy

For the aspic:

>2 cups duck stock
>¼ cup sherry
>1 tablespoon unflavored gelatin

For the final garnish:

>½ orange, sliced paper thin
>1 green onion top, slivered lengthwise

To prepare ducks, remove necks and giblets and sort into two piles, one with necks and gizzards, the other with livers and hearts. Set aside. Remove fat from cavities and set aside in a third pile. Skin and then bone ducks following procedure described in **galantine of turkey** recipe (see page 44) with the following exception: duck legs are not so splintery as turkey legs, so they may be carefully boned and the meat used in the forcemeat. Add all the boned meat to the pile of livers and hearts. Add wing tips, carcasses, and leg and thigh bones to the pile of necks and gizzards. Set the best looking skin aside for encasing the galantine along with some neck skin for patching any holes. Add the other skin to the pile of duck fat from the cavities and use all this to render duck fat for other uses.

Place duck breasts, livers, hearts, and boned meat in nonreactive container. Sprinkle red wine and freshly ground black pepper over top. Place duck skin on top and marinate in refrigerator overnight.

To make stock, place bones, necks, and gizzards in a large pot, breaking up carcasses to fit. Pour in water, adding more if liquid does not cover bones. Bring to a boil and skim occasionally for 10 minutes. Add remaining stock ingredients, reduce heat, and simmer 1½ hours. Don't let stock boil or aspic will be cloudy. Pour stock through a strainer lined with clean cloth into a bowl. Let cool to room temperature, cover with plastic wrap, and refrigerate overnight.

On the second day, make the forcemeat. Grind duck meat except the breasts, hearts, and livers together with other meats and onion. Add seasoning ingredients for forcemeat and the marinating liquid. Using hands, blend well. Don't use an electric mixer, as duck meat will become tough if overworked.

Preheat oven to 350 degrees.

To assemble galantine, you will need two 2 quart loaf pans. Line one with duck skin, patching any holes with neck skin. Pack half the forcemeat into the bottom. Cut hearts and livers crosswise. Cut breasts lengthwise into 4 strips each. Arrange liver, heart, and breast pieces down center. Fill with remaining forcemeat, patting into corners to eliminate air pockets. Fold skin over top, pushing edges together to enclose the forcemeat. Place second loaf pan on top of first, hold together, and invert so galantine lands breast side up in second pan.

To cook, place in oven and bake 1¾ hours, or until an instant reading meat thermometer registers 152 degrees. Remove, cool to room temperature, cover, and refrigerate overnight.

On the third day, remove stock from refrigerator, scrape fat off surface, and pour or scoop 2 cups stock into a clean pot, leaving behind sediment on the bottom. Discard sediment. Set pot over medium heat and bring to a boil. Remove ¼ cup to a small bowl as soon as liquid state is reached. Add sherry to the small bowl. When stock is boiling, dissolve gelatin in liquid in the small bowl and whisk into boiling stock. Immediately remove from heat, whisk a little more, then pour through a strainer lined with clean cloth into a clean bowl. Set aside to cool.

To finish, unmold galantine, wipe off excess fat, and dry with paper toweling. Place on a platter. Decoratively arrange orange slices and slivers of green onion on top, using this opportunity to cover any holes in duck skin. Return to refrigerator while preparing aspic.

The aspic stock should be at the point of setting but still barely liquid. If not, set the bowl in a larger bowl filled with ice and stir aspic. This is the tricky part: if aspic becomes set and no longer pourable, you have to start over by remelting and cooling it again; if aspic is not set enough, it will not glaze the galantine. It is just right when it coats a cold metal spoon. When aspic reaches the correct consistency, pour ¼ cup over galantine and chill until set. Add 2 more coats in the same way. Pour the aspic remaining after the third coat into a small rectangular container and chill until set, about 1 hour. Galantine will keep wrapped and refrigerated up to 5 days.

To serve, unmold the aspic from the rectangular container by partially immersing in hot water for 2 seconds. Cover with a plate larger than the container and invert. Cut aspic into ¼ inch cubes. Place galantine on a clean serving platter and surround with aspic cubes. Accompany with warm French bread and a bowl of green Sicilian olives.

GALANTINE DE BOEUF
CALIFORNIENNE

Mediterranean flavors—garlic, lemon, and olive oil—harmoniously mingle with Oriental—soy, ginger, and coriander—in our contemporary interpretation of a classic galantine of beef.

——————— Dinner for 4 or a buffet platter for 8 ———————

1 large flank steak, not too lean, about 1¾ pounds

For the marinade:

> **2 cups red wine**
> **⅔ cup soy sauce**
> **1 tablespoon lemon juice**
> **½ cup olive oil**
> **1 inch fresh ginger root, peeled and grated**
> **1 little hot chili, minced, or ½ teaspoon red chili flakes**
> **4 garlic cloves, peeled and slivered**
> **1 bay leaf, crumbled**
> **6 sprigs fresh coriander**

For the stuffing:

> **1 pound fresh spinach**
> **1 medium carrot, peeled and cut into ¹⁄₁₆ inch dice**
> **⅛ pound fresh mushrooms, preferably shiitake, sliced thin**

Have butcher butterfly flank steak parallel to grain, or do it yourself using a chef's knife. Lay steak out flat and cut through thickness of meat holding knife lengthwise, parallel to the grain. Stop ½ inch from slicing clear through meat. Set aside.

Mix ingredients for marinade in a nonreactive container just large enough to hold butterflied flank steak opened out. Place meat in marinade and set aside unrefrigerated 15 to 30 minutes, turning two or three times.

To prepare stuffing, cut spinach leaves crosswise into ½ inch strips and chop stems. Immerse spinach in plenty of cold water, let sit a few seconds so dirt settles to bottom, then lift out into a colander. Repeat with fresh water. Put wet spinach into a large nonreactive skillet or pot along with diced carrot and sliced mushrooms. Stir over medium heat 2 or 3 minutes, until spinach is wilted. Drain in a colander and press out all excess liquid with a wooden spoon. Let cool in colander.

Preheat oven to 475 degrees. To assemble, lift flank steak out of marinade and place, opened out, on counter. Spread stuffing over meat and moisten with 2 tablespoons marinade. Roll flank steak lengthwise, with the grain, and tie at 1½ inch intervals, starting in center and working out to ends. Tuck in ends and tie with one long string end to end.

To make a sauce, cook remaining marinade in a nonreactive pot over medium high heat until reduced by half, about 45 minutes.

To cook galantine, place in a roasting pan in the preheated oven. After 10 minutes, reduce oven heat to 350 degrees and cook 20 minutes more, or until an instant reading meat thermometer registers 135 degrees. Remove galantine from oven and let rest in a warm place 15 minutes so juices can settle into meat. Or cool completely, wrap, and refrigerate overnight. Add juices collected in bottom of roasting pan to reduced marinade sauce.

To serve hot, slice ⅜ inch thick, moisten slices with sauce, and accompany with remaining sauce. To serve cold, slice thinner and arrange on a buffet platter, moistened with sauce.

TERRINE DE POISSONS

Terrine de poissons can be varied in many ways, depending on your momentary whim for color and composition. The terrine may be lined with salmon fillets or sorrel leaves as well as sole fillets. The mousseline may be of sole or salmon or smoked trout. The center may be scallops, salmon fillets, or a mousseline of sorrel. The terrine described in the recipe below, masked with a green mayonnaise, alternates colors: green, white, and pink, and also textures: smooth and coarse. If you have a food processor or electric blender, it is not difficult to make. Since the delicate flavor of this terrine depends on pristinely fresh fish, it should be consumed within 2 days to be at its best.

──────────── For a 4 pound terrine ────────────

For lining the terrine:

　　　2 pounds sole fillets
　　　juice of 1 lemon
　　　1 teaspoon salt
　　　½ teaspoon cayenne

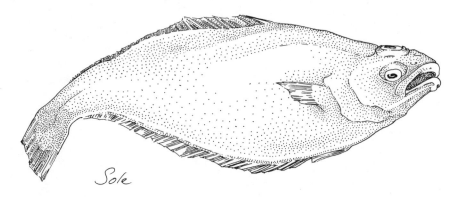

Sole

For the center:

>2/3 pound salmon fillet
>2 to 4 chard leaves, enough to spread over surface of
>terrine twice

For the mousseline:

>1 1/2 pounds salmon meat, skinned, well chilled
>2 egg whites, chilled
>1 cup heavy cream, chilled
>3 tablespoons lemon juice
>1 tablespoon salt
>1/2 teaspoon cayenne

Optional aspic glaze:

>1/2 cup dry white wine
>1 tablespoon lemon juice
>1 cup water
>1 tablespoon unflavored gelatin
>a few sprigs fresh dill
>a few paper thin slices of lemon

To prepare sole and salmon fillets, place in a glass or other nonreactive container. Pour lemon juice over them and sprinkle with salt and cayenne. Turn fillets to coat with seasoning on all sides. Set aside in refrigerator to marinate.

To prepare chard leaves, hold leaves by stems and dip into boiling water. Remove immediately and cut out white ribs. Set aside.

To prepare mousseline, swirl ingredients in a food processor until smooth but not stiff, about 30 seconds. Set aside.

Preheat oven to 350 degrees. To assemble, line a 2 quart capacity ceramic or enamel terrine with sole fillets. Pack terrine with half the salmon mousseline, spread half the wilted chard over surface, place salmon fillet down center, top with remaining chard, then with rest of salmon mousseline. Finish with sole fillets on top. Cover with foil, pinching around edges to seal.

To cook, bake in a *bain-marie* 1 hour, or until an instant reading meat thermometer registers 115 degrees. Remove from oven and cool to room temperature. Pour off excess liquid, weight with a few cans, and refrigerate overnight.

To make the optional aspic glaze, place wine, lemon juice, and ¾ cup water in a small nonreactive pan and bring to a boil. In a small bowl, dissolve gelatin in ¼ cup water, whisk into the boiling liquid, and immediately remove from heat. Whisk again and pour through a strainer lined with clean cloth into a clean bowl. Set aside to cool. Remove terrine from refrigerator, peel away foil, and pour off excess liquid. Pat top dry and clean rim of terrine. Arrange dill sprigs and lemon slices on top, then pour aspic over all, rearranging dill and lemon if necessary. Chill several hours until aspic is set.

To serve, leave in the terrine if aspic glaze has been added; it is almost impossible to unmold with the aspic intact. If aspic glaze has not been used, unmold or leave in the terrine and spread a thin layer of green mayonnaise over the top, then sprinkle with the grated rind of 1 lemon. In either case, cut into ½ inch thick slices and accompany with a bowl of green mayonnaise.

GREEN MAYONNAISE:

2 pounds fresh spinach
4 egg yolks
1 teaspoon Dijon mustard
1 tablespoon lemon juice
½ teaspoon salt
2 cups olive or peanut oil, or a mixture
1 tablespoon chopped fresh dill, or 1 teaspoon dried
¼ cup chopped fresh parsley

To prepare spinach, cut leaves crosswise into ¼ inch strips; discard stems. Immerse in cold water, let dirt settle a few seconds, lift spinach out, and repeat with clean water. Remove spinach to a medium size nonreactive pot and stir over medium heat until completely wilted. Drain and set aside to cool.

In a food processor, or using an electric mixer or wire whisk, mix egg yolks with mustard, lemon juice, and salt. Slowly beat in oil, starting with 1 teaspoon at a time and working up to a slow, steady stream. Remove mayonnaise to a bowl. Squeeze all liquid out of spinach and purée in a food processor or mince with a chef's knife. Stir spinach, dill, and parsley into mayonnaise. Add more salt and lemon juice to taste. Chill.

TERRINE DE LÉGUMES

Terrine de légumes *is our contribution to modern pâté making.
We turned up our noses at vegetarian pâtés, all of which seemed
like an infelicitous compromise on a good idea, until we came
across Vera Gewanter's recipe for lentil pâté in her book A
Passion for Vegetables. Eureka! puréed légume is, of course,
the perfect substitute for meat. We have added a lining of grape
leaves, a spinach mousseline center studded with sun dried tomatoes, and an accompanying yogurt and mint sauce for color
and taste variety. French lentils are preferred for their nuttier
flavor, but regular lentils will do: cook them only 20 to 25
minutes. If you are not making a strictly vegetarian dish, chicken
stock may be used instead of water for an extra flavor boost.*

For a 4½ pound terrine

For the force"meat":

    1 pound dried French lentils
    1 small onion, peeled and roughly chopped
    6 garlic cloves, peeled and roughly chopped
    ½ pound fresh tomatoes, preferably Roma, roughly
        chopped
    1 bay leaf
    1 heaping teaspoon fresh thyme leaves, or ½ teaspoon
        dried
    1 teaspoon salt
    5 cups water

For seasoning:

    ½ cup heavy cream
    2 eggs
    1 teaspoon paprika
    ¼ teaspoon cayenne
    1 teaspoon salt
    juice of 1 lemon

For the center:

> 1½ pounds fresh spinach
> ½ cup ricotta cheese
> ⅓ cup heavy cream
> ¼ teaspoon salt
> ¼ teaspoon grated nutmeg

> ¼ pound Italian sun dried tomatoes

> 8 to 10 grape leaves, depending on size, for lining the
>   terrine

To make forcemeat, place ingredients in a nonreactive pot. Bring to a boil, partially cover, and simmer 35 minutes, or until liquid is absorbed and lentils are quite soft. Remove bay leaf and purée the mixture in a food processor or blender. Or, push through a food mill. Beat in ½ cup cream, eggs, paprika, cayenne, salt, and lemon juice. Set aside.

To prepare center, cut spinach leaves into ½ inch strips crosswise; fine chop stems. Plunge into plenty of cold water, let sit a few seconds so dirt will settle to bottom, lift out, and repeat with fresh water. Lift out into a colander. Place spinach in a large nonreactive pot over medium heat and stir until completely wilted. Drain in a colander. When cool enough to handle, squeeze out excess water, then purée in a food processor along with ricotta cheese and ⅓ cup cream. Or chop spinach fine, then beat in ricotta cheese and cream. Season with salt and nutmeg. Set aside.

Preheat oven to 375 degrees. To assemble, line a 2 quart terrine or loaf pan with grape leaves placed inside up. Place half the lentil mixture on the bottom. Place the spinach mixture on top of that. Arrange sun dried tomatoes down the center, then top with remaining lentil mixture. Enclose with grape leaves, then cover with aluminum foil, pinching around edges to seal. Pierce foil in three places to allow steam to escape.

To cook, place in oven without a *bain-marie* and bake 1 hour and 15 minutes, or until an instant reading meat thermometer registers 162 degrees. Remove, cool to room temperature, and refrigerate overnight, up to 2 days. Will keep up to 5 days.

To serve, unmold terrine, cut into ½ inch thick slices, and accompany with yogurt and mint sauce.

YOGURT AND MINT SAUCE:

Place 1 quart yogurt in a strainer lined with clean cloth and leave 2 hours to drain off liquid, called the whey. Place the drained yogurt in a bowl and stir in 3 tablespoons chopped fresh mint leaves or 2 teaspoons dried.

PÂTÉ DE CANARD SAUVAGE

One year we had the good fortune to be presented with some wild ducks just in time to create a pâté for the wedding of our friends Bert and Geneviève. Wild ducks are not generally available, but should you acquire some, this is a good way to treat them, and so we offer this recipe as a culinary quip. To begin, hang by the neck three wild ducks, spoonbills or mallards, in a dry and well ventilated spot which maintains a temperature between 34 and 40 degrees. After 5 days, pluck and dress them. Domestic Muscovy ducks, whose rich and slightly gamy flavor approaches that of wild duck, can be successfully used instead.

──────────── For a 3 pound pâté ────────────

3 wild ducks
2 tablespoons dry Madeira wine
freshly ground black pepper

For the stock:

the duck skins, wings, bones, and gizzards
1 onion, unpeeled and quartered
2 sprigs fresh thyme, or $1/4$ teaspoon dried
1 bay leaf
1 cup white wine
6 cups water

For the forcemeat:

3 tablespoons butter
2 medium Red Delicious apples, unpeeled, cored, and roughly chopped
3 large shallots, peeled and roughly chopped
$1/2$ teaspoon fresh thyme leaves, or $1/8$ teaspoon dried
$1/2$ teaspoon chopped fresh sage leaves, or $1/8$ teaspoon dried

3 tablespoons butter
the duck livers and hearts
2 domestic duck livers
freshly ground black pepper
1/4 cup brandy

1 pound veal
1/4 pound pork butt

For seasoning:

1/2 teaspoon fresh thyme leaves, or a pinch of dried
1/2 teaspoon minced fresh sage leaves, or a pinch of
   dried
2 teaspoons salt
1 egg
1/2 cup wild duck stock

3/4 pound bacon, blanched 3 minutes, for lining the
   terrine
1 bay leaf

To prepare ducks, remove skins and wings and set aside. Bone ducks in the same manner as described for **galantine of turkey** (see recipe page 44). Set bones aside with skins and wings. Marinate breasts of 2 ducks in Madeira and pepper and set aside. Set rest of duck meat aside.

To prepare stock, place stock ingredients in a nonreactive pot, adding more water to cover if necessary. Bring to a boil and simmer 1 1/2 hours. Pour through a strainer lined with clean cloth into a bowl and set aside to cool. When tepid, ladle fat off top.

In a sauté pan, heat 3 tablespoons butter until foaming. Add apples, shallots, and herbs and cook over medium heat until quite soft. Set aside.

In another sauté pan, heat 3 tablespoons butter until foaming. Add domestic duck livers and cook over medium heat 4 minutes. Add livers and hearts of wild ducks and black pepper to taste. Continue cooking until livers are firm but still pink in centers, about 5 minutes more. Raise heat, add brandy and ignite it, shaking pan back and forth until flames subside. Remove to a bowl to cool 15 minutes.

To prepare forcemeat, use small grinder plate and grind together apples, shallots, livers, hearts, duck meat except marinating breasts, veal, and pork, pouring through ½ cup of the strained duck stock and any juices accumulated in sauté pan and bowl. Add seasoning ingredients and the Madeira from marinating breasts. Mix well with hands.

Preheat oven to 325 degrees. To assemble, line a 2 quart terrine or loaf pan with blanched bacon strips. Pack in half the forcemeat, arrange whole breasts down the center, and fill with remaining forcemeat. Place bay leaf on top and cover with bacon strips, enclosing neatly. Cover with lid or foil.

To cook, bake in a *bain-marie* 1 hour. Remove lid or foil and continue cooking 30 to 45 minutes, until an instant reading meat thermometer registers 165 degrees. Remove, cool to room temperature, cover and refrigerate 2 to 3 days to allow flavors to blend.

To serve, unmold or leave in the terrine and accompany with pickled ginger, oysters on the half shell, and warm French bread.

Bay leaves

PICKLED GINGER:

Peel 1 pound fresh ginger root and slice paper thin. Place in a 1 quart nonreactive storage container and set aside. In a nonreactive pot, bring to a boil 1 cup rice wine vinegar and 1 cup mirin (sweet rice wine). Boil 1 minute, then pour over ginger slices. Refrigerate 3 days before using.

SAUSAGES

*T*he origin of sausage making is not known, although there is evidence of meat-stuffed intestinal casings in the Mesopotamian cuisine of 4000 B.C. We may conjecture that the first sausages were minced and salted pork scraps stuffed into the handy package provided by the pig's intestine, perhaps made to use up fat trimmings and bits of meat left after the butchering of a hog. Today, sausages range from simply ground and seasoned pork to refined and manipulated concoctions of meats and seasonings, some entirely without pork. They are divided into two kinds. **Preserved sausages** such as salami and smoked sausage, called *saucissons secs* and *saucissons fumés* in French charcuterie, are made to be stored. They require the curing effects of both salting (including nitrates and nitrites to protect against botulinum and other anaerobic organisms) and desiccating (air drying and/or smoking). **Fresh sausages,** *saucisses* and *cervelas* in French charcuterie, are meant to be consumed within a week, and therefore may be made with less salt and without nitrite as long as they are refrigerated. Moreover, since the meat is not dehydrated, less added fat is needed for succulence.

Most of the recipes in this chapter are for fresh sausages designed with a minimum of salts and added fat. Exceptions are *boudin blanc* which requires extra fat to achieve its creamy texture, and beef salami which is a preserved sausage and requires saltpeter.

PROCEDURES AND INGREDIENTS

To achieve a moist and tender cooked sausage, the **meat** should be lightly marbled with fat and not gristly. **Pork butt** is the best combination of noncartilaginous meat and just enough fat to produce succulent sausages without adding much fat. In French charcuterie, the throat or neck meat is esteemed for sausage as well as pâté, but it is not part of American butchery.

The **tenderloin** and both **end cuts of pork loin** are also first choice meats for fresh sausage. However, the center cut pork loin is too hard and too lean for sausage meat, even with fat added. Picnic trim from the leg of pork is too gristly except for sausages like *boudins blancs* or frankfurters, which are finely ground twice and twice cooked.

Other meat preferences indicated in the recipes, such as **lamb shoulder** for lamb *crépinettes* and **chicken breast including skin** for *crépinettes* and *boudins* are based on the same considerations of texture and balance between meat and fat.

When **fat** is added, it should be flavorful and firm. Pork **fatback** in slabs or the hard, thick **fat from outside the butt** and **loin** are best for sausages. **Leaf lard,** the hard fat from around the kidneys, is also suitable but is rarely found in American butcher shops, except by special order.

Fresh pork belly may be substituted for fatback or butt trim in sausages. However, salt pork, which is cured pork belly, does not work well for fresh sausage because it is chewy unless cooked for many hours. Soft fat, such as the trim from the leg or interior of the shoulder, will make the sausage mushy. We prefer to use soft fat trimming by rendering it into lard.

To avoid mashing them, have meats and fat cold when cut and when stuffed. It is advantageous to chill sausage stuffing 30 minutes before filling casings, but not much longer or it will become too firm and be more difficult to stuff into the casings.

When ground meats should not be overworked, to avoid toughening, directions in the recipes indicate **mixing** seasonings in, preferably with hands and just enough to distribute everything evenly. When ground meats need to be tenderized, directions indicate **beating** seasonings in, either with an electric mixer for 1 full minute or else by vigorous kneading with hands for 2 or 3 minutes. Directions indicate **whipping,** preferably with an electric mixer for 1½ minutes, when stuffing needs to be aerated and fluffed up.

Sausage is usually **encased,** though it need not be. To **prepare casing** for stuffing, cut into convenient lengths and rinse salt off outside. Fit one end over water tap and run cold water through to rinse out inside.

In addition to rinsing out salt, this step makes it much easier to slide the casing onto the stuffing horn.

To **fill casing,** slide a length of rinsed casing onto the stuffing horn or funnel tube and feed in sausage meat until the first bit comes out the end. Push out the air bubble preceding the meat, then tie a knot in the end of the casing. Continue pushing sausage through, in small amounts to avoid overstuffing the feeder and clogging the whole process. If using an automatic stuffer, control speed and degree of filling casing with one hand as you feed with the other. If sausage is to be tied into links, casing should be almost, but not quite, filled, with just enough play to allow twisting. If sausage is to be coiled or tied in one large link, casing should be full almost to bursting. In any case, work out air pockets with non-feeding hand as you go. This is a little like patting your head and rubbing your stomach at the same time; it can be done with concentration and some practice. Stop 3 inches short of the end, slide the casing off the horn, and knot the end. The last bit of sausage meat may be pushed through the grinder into the casing by sending a piece of fatback through at the end.

Casings vary widely in degree of toughness or tenderness. Tough ones feel rubbery and thick. They should be discarded when detected as they are unpleasant to eat.

There are several ways **to tie off sausages.** They may be twisted into links (not very satisfactory, they come undone) or tied off with individual pieces of string (laborious). Best is the professional loop de loop braid (see pages 72–73). Pinch sausage between thumb and forefinger as far up from end as the intended length of each link, e.g., 5 inches from end for 5 inch links. With second hand, twist sausage an equal length farther down to make second link. You now have two links attached to a length of untied sausage. With second hand, bring untied length up and over at spot where thumb and forefinger are still holding; lift thumb to include new piece in same pinch. With second hand still, reach through loop you have just created and pull sausage through just enough to make a new loop. Pinch new loop between thumb and forefinger of second hand and release grasp on first loop, freeing first hand. With first hand, bring untied length of sausage up and over new loop. Continue until length is used up.

Sausage may also be encased in **caul.** The French term for these pretty parcels is *gayettes* or sometimes *boulettes* when the shape is rounded,

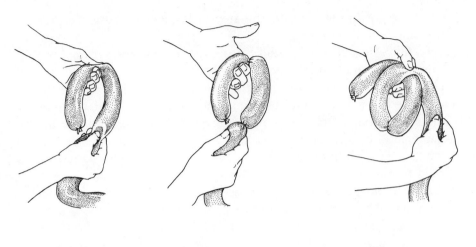

| *Pinch* | *Twist* | *Wrap up* |

or *crépinettes,* after the French for caul, *crépine,* when they are flat patties. The English term is "faggots," and the Americans have no word. We use the French term *crépinettes.* Any fresh sausage may be wrapped in caul if gut is unavailable or not feasible to use. However, since the filling is not as tightly packed nor as aerated in caul, the texture of the sausage is somewhat looser, or wetter. Caul is too perishable to be substituted for gut casing when sausage is to be treated for keeping.

Except for those wrapped in caul, fresh sausages which have had liquid such as wine or beer added are **hung** in an airy place cooler than 60 degrees for a short time. The hanging makes the meat firm and drains off excess liquid which would otherwise steam and toughen the meat during cooking. If there is not a convenient cool place to hang the sausages, they may be placed on racks in the refrigerator, uncovered and not touching each other. Be sure to place a drip pan underneath in either case.

Sausages are always **chilled** at least overnight to allow flavors to blend, either after they have hung or after they have been poached. Place hung sausages in one layer on a nonreactive surface, cover with wax paper, and refrigerate overnight.

After sausages are chilled, lift out of rendered juices, pat dry, and **store** wrapped in wax or butcher paper in the refrigerator. Avoid using

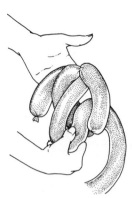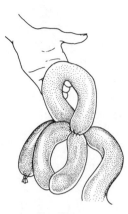

Pull through   *Pinch and twist*   *Start again*

plastic wrap; because it is nonporous, it prevents air circulation around the sausages and therefore accelerates spoilage. Freezing is the least satisfactory way to store fresh sausages. It diminishes both color and sweetness of flavor. Halve quantities given in the recipes if the quantity is too much to use without freezing.

To **poach** sausages, gently lower them into a large pot of boiling water, reduce heat to just below a simmer, and cook as directed, turning once. Carefully remove cooked sausages from water, they break easily at this point, and cool to room temperature before chilling. Poached sausage may be eaten cold or can be heated by sautéing, grilling, or steaming.

Sausages are sometimes partially boiled to set the meat before finishing on the grill or *en casserole*. To **parboil** sausages, lower chilled sausages into boiling water, reduce heat to below a simmer, and cook 5 minutes for sheep casing links, 10 minutes for hog casing links, and 15 minutes for beef casing links. Gently remove and cool 15 minutes, up to 2 hours, before grilling or adding to composed dish. Sausages won't be as juicy if they are refrigerated again.

To **sauté** sausages, place in a skillet, with or without butter as directed, and cook over medium heat. Reduce heat to medium low if sausages are browning too fast. Leave skillet uncovered so sausages will not steam and toughen. A small amount of water or wine may be added to help reduce the popping and sizzling.

To **grill** sausages, prepare mesquite or other wood and let coals burn until white all over with some spots of red showing, 20 to 30 minutes depending on size of fire and type of wood. If using charcoal briquets, preheat fire 10 to 15 minutes longer to burn off ill tasting petroleum contained in briquets. If grill is large enough, arrange sausages on the grill around the edges of the fire rather than directly over coals. This method of indirect heat grilling eliminates flaming from rendering fat and produces more even cooking. If grilling directly over coals, have a spray bottle handy to douse flames.

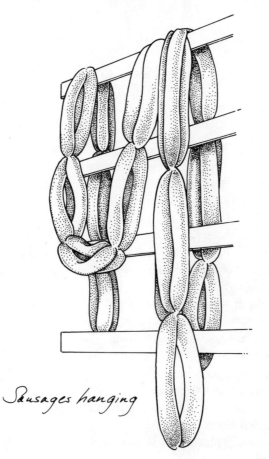

Sausages hanging

CRÉPINETTES

Crépinettes are the easiest sausage to make. You may even purchase already ground pork from the butcher, omit the fatback in the recipe, and hand mince the chicken breast. As in all the recipes, the spinach should be fresh or the vegetable flavor won't be strong enough. Lacking a supply of caul fat to wrap the sausage meat in, form into a patty and fry, using a little butter in this case.

——————— For 16 sausages, about 4 ounces each ———————

1 pound fresh spinach
2 tablespoons butter

For grinding, medium plate:
> **2½ pounds pork butt**
> **1¼ pounds boned chicken breasts, including skin**
> **¼ pound fatback**

For seasoning:
> **1 slightly rounded teaspoon pâté spice (see page 5)**
> **¼ teaspoon grated nutmeg**
> **1 teaspoon black pepper**
> **¼ teaspoon cayenne**
> **2 teaspoons salt**

> **½ to ⅔ pound caul fat**
> **16 fresh basil or tarragon leaves, or 16 small dried bay**
> **leaves**

Shred spinach leaves crosswise into ½ inch strips and chop stems. Immerse in cold water, let sit a few seconds while dirt sinks to bottom, lift out, and repeat with fresh water. Lift into a colander after second wash and drain 1 minute. Melt butter in nonreactive pot, add spinach, and stir over medium low heat until completely wilted. Remove from heat and let cool completely. Spinach should not be warm when added to meats or sausage will spoil faster. When cool, drain off liquid, but do not press dry.

Mix ground meats and fat with cooled spinach and seasoning ingredients. Chill sausage at least 2 hours, up to 3 days, before wrapping in caul fat.

To wrap, lay caul out on counter and divide into 4 inch squares. Place herb leaf in center of each square, top with ¼ pound sausage, and wrap neatly. Will keep wrapped in wax or butcher paper and refrigerated up to 3 days.

To cook, place in an unheated, ungreased skillet over medium low heat or place on grill over a prepared fire. Cook 15 minutes, turn, and cook 10 minutes more. If grilling directly over coals, don't forget to have a spray bottle handy.

LAMB CRÉPINETTES

Cooked to a turn at medium rare, spicy and sweet lamb crépinettes add an unusual Middle Eastern touch to a mixed grill.
Serve leftovers cold, with **yogurt and mint sauce** (see page
62) and sliced cucumbers. If currants and Anaheim chilies are
not available, substitute golden raisins and green bell pepper.

──────────── For 14 sausages, about 4 ounces each ────────────

2 tablespoons unsalted butter
½ cup currants
2 tablespoons pine nuts

For grinding, small plate:

3 pounds lamb shoulder or stew meat

For seasoning:

1 teaspoon minced fresh little chili
2 long green Anaheim chilies, minced
1 tablespoon minced garlic
1 tablespoon fresh thyme leaves, or 1 teaspoon dried
¼ cup chopped fresh parsley
1 teaspoon cayenne
2 teaspoons salt
⅓ cup olive oil
⅓ cup red wine

½ pound caul fat

Heat butter in a skillet, then add currants and pine nuts. Sauté
until currants are plumped up and pine nuts are slightly browned. Cool
10 minutes. Add to lamb along with seasoning ingredients and mix well
with hands. Wrap in 3 inch squares of caul. Will keep wrapped in wax
or butcher paper and refrigerated up to 4 days.

To cook, sauté in a little butter or grill 15 minutes, turning once.

TOULOUSE SAUSAGE

Although there is nothing spectacular in the seasoning ingredients, the harmonizing flavors of salt, sweet, and pepper make Toulouse sausage taste more complex than it is. Coiled Toulouse is often skewered crosswise and grilled in a piece. Not encased, Toulouse sausage may be used, with or without embellishment, in any recipe calling for sausage meat. The sugar and saltpeter which give Toulouse sausage its characteristic taste may be omitted if you do not mind sacrificing rosy color.

——————————— For 3 sausage coils, about 1½ pounds each ———————————

For grinding, large plate:
> 4½ pounds pork butt
> ⅓ pound fatback

For seasoning:
> ½ teaspoon grated nutmeg
> ½ teaspoon cayenne
> ½ teaspoon white pepper
> ½ teaspoon black pepper
> 1 teaspoon sugar
> 1 teaspoon saltpeter
> 2 teaspoons salt

Nutmeg and grater

6 feet hog casing, in 2 foot lengths, rinsed

With hands, mix seasonings with ground pork and fat, enough to distribute seasonings thoroughly, but without kneading meat. Stuff into hog casing, feeding sausage into grinder in dollops to avoid smashing meat. Wind into a coil or tie at 4½ inch intervals and refrigerate at least overnight, up to 2 days, to allow flavors to blend. Will keep wrapped in wax or butcher paper and refrigerated up to 7 days.

To cook, sauté in butter or grill 20 minutes. Or parboil 10 minutes and add to a composed dish for the last 20 to 30 minutes of cooking.

■ ■

SWEET ITALIAN SAUSAGE

Italian fresh sausages, although not as varied in textures and flavors, vie with their French counterparts in robust tastiness. This and the three following range from mildly sweet, which describes the fennel flavor in the sweet Italian, to assertively spicy. All are suitable for pasta sauces, pizzas, and sausage stuffings.

—————————— For 20 sausages, about 4 ounces each ——————————

For grinding, medium plate:
> **5 pounds pork butt**

For seasoning:
> **1 tablespoon minced garlic**
> **¼ cup chopped fresh parsley**
> **1 tablespoon chopped fresh oregano leaves, or 1 teaspoon dried**
> **1 tablespoon fresh thyme leaves, or 1 teaspoon dried**
> **1 tablespoon fennel seed**
> **1 teaspoon black pepper**
> **½ teaspoon cayenne**
> **1 tablespoon salt**
> **1 cup white wine, not too dry**

> **9 feet hog casing, in 3 foot lengths, rinsed**

Mix seasonings except wine with ground pork. Add wine and mix in. Stuff into hog casing, tie at 4½ inch intervals, and hang for 1 hour. Refrigerate overnight to allow flavors to blend. Will keep up to 5 days wrapped in wax or butcher paper and refrigerated.

To cook, sauté in a little olive oil over medium heat or grill 18 to 20 minutes, turning to brown all around.

SPICY GARLIC SAUSAGE

Dried chili may be substituted when fresh is not available, but the flavor of the sausage will vary accordingly: fresh chili tastes like a vegetable while dried chili tastes like a spice.

——————————— For 20 sausages, about 4 ounces each ———————————

For grinding, medium plate:
5 pounds pork butt

For seasoning:
**3 tablespoons fresh hot chili, minced,
    or 2 teaspoons dried red chili flakes
2 tablespoons minced garlic
1 tablespoon chopped fresh sage leaves,
    or 1 teaspoon dried
¼ cup chopped fresh parsley
2 teaspoons black pepper
½ teaspoon cayenne
1 tablespoon salt
1 cup robust red wine**

9 feet hog casing, in 3 foot lengths, rinsed

Mix seasonings except wine with ground pork. Add wine and mix in. Stuff into hog casing, tie at 4½ inch intervals, and hang for 1 hour. Refrigerate overnight to allow flavors to blend. Will keep up to 5 days wrapped in wax or butcher paper and refrigerated.

To cook, sauté in a little olive oil over medium heat or grill 18 to 20 minutes, turning to brown all around.

■ ■

TUSCAN SAUSAGE

To savor its wonderful aroma, which is lost during cooking, we normally reserve basil for a garnishing herb. However, in this sausage it works well with the tomato and the cheese to accentuate the taste of Summer. The addition of mozzarella cheese and the absence of any alcohol make Tuscan sausages more perishable than other fresh sausages. They should be eaten within 4 days.

―――――――――― For 20 sausages, about 4 ounces each ――――――――――

For grinding, medium plate:
   5 pounds pork butt

For seasoning:
   ½ pound fresh tomatoes
   2 ounces mozzarella cheese
   2 teaspoons minced garlic
   2 tablespoons chopped fresh basil leaves
   1 tablespoon chopped fresh parsley
   2 teaspoons black pepper
   2 teaspoons salt

   9 feet hog casing, in 3 foot lengths, rinsed

Peel tomatoes with a sharp knife. Don't parboil them to loosen skins or they will be too soft. Seed, cut into ¼ inch dice, and add to ground pork. Cut mozzarella into ¼ inch dice and add to ground pork. Add remaining seasonings and mix well. Stuff into hog casing and tie at 4½ inch intervals. Refrigerate overnight to allow flavors to blend. Will keep up to 4 days wrapped in wax or butcher paper and refrigerated.

To cook, sauté in a little olive oil over medium heat or grill 18 to 20 minutes, turning once to brown all around.

ITALIAN PARMESAN SAUSAGE

Called luganega *in Italian, this mild pork and Parmesan cheese sausage is one of the favorites at Pig-by-the-Tail. It should be eaten fresh, within 3 days, before the cheese causes the flavor to "go off."*

──────────── For 5 pounds coiled sausage ────────────

For grinding, large plate:

5 pounds pork butt, well trimmed

For seasoning:

1⅓ cups, loosely packed, grated Parmesan cheese
1 tablespoon finely chopped garlic
**1 tablespoon chopped fresh oregano leaves,
    or 1 teaspoon dried**
2 teaspoons black pepper
2 teaspoons salt
¼ cup white wine

6 feet hog casing, in 3 foot lengths, rinsed

Flowering oregano

Mix seasonings except wine with ground pork. Add wine and mix in. Stuff into hog casing and coil. Refrigerate overnight to allow flavors to blend. Will keep up to 3 days wrapped in wax or butcher paper and refrigerated.

To cook, sauté in a little olive oil over medium heat or grill 18 to 20 minutes, turning once to brown all around.

■ ■

SAUCISSE POLONAISE

Chooch's version of kielbasa is lighter and less cured tasting than the more familiar processed Polish sausage of that name. Its faintly garlicky, smoky flavor goes well with cabbage, potato, or white bean dishes.

——————————— For 20 sausages, about 4 ounces each ———————————

For grinding, medium plate:

> 2½ pounds pork butt
> 2½ pounds ground beef chuck
> ⅓ pound smoked ham

For the blender or food processor:

> 8 garlic cloves, peeled and mashed
> 1 bottle full flavored beer, not dark

For seasoning:

> ½ teaspoon dried sage
> 1 teaspoon dried mustard
> ½ teaspoon grated mace
> 1 teaspoon ground coriander seed
> 1½ teaspoons black pepper
> 1 teaspoon sugar
> 2 teaspoons salt

> 9 feet hog casing, in 3 foot lengths, rinsed

Mix ground meats with blended garlic and beer. Add seasonings and mix in. Stuff into hog casing, tie at 4½ inch intervals, and hang 1 hour. Refrigerate overnight to allow flavors to blend. Will keep up to 5 days wrapped in wax or butcher paper and refrigerated.

To cook, sauté in butter or grill 18 to 20 minutes, turning to brown all around. Or parboil 10 minutes, then add to a composed dish for the last 30 minutes of cooking time.

CHAMPAGNE SAUSAGE

These are elegant link sausages, especially good for cocktail hors d'oeuvre or as a garnishing sausage for egg or fowl dishes. The meat may be all pork butt if pork tenderloin is not available. The Champagne should be extra dry, not brut.

——————————— For 30 sausages, about 1½ ounces each ———————————

For grinding, small plate:

1½ pounds pork tenderloin
1½ pounds pork butt
¼ pound fatback

For seasoning:

2 eggs
1 teaspoon minced garlic
1 teaspoon pâté spice
1 teaspoon grated nutmeg
½ teaspoon white pepper
1 teaspoon salt
¼ cup extra dry Champagne

12 feet sheep casing, in 3 to 4 foot lengths, rinsed

With an electric mixer, mix seasonings except Champagne with ground meat and fat. Beat in Champagne. Stuff into sheep casing, tie at 4 inch intervals, and hang for 1 hour. Refrigerate overnight to allow flavors to blend. Will keep 6 days wrapped in wax or butcher paper and refrigerated.

To cook, sauté in butter over medium heat 10 minutes, turning to brown all around. Or parboil 5 minutes then grill 5 minutes.

CREOLE SAUSAGE

*Thyme, chilies, and spices, characteristic tastes of Creole cooking, are given an added zing with a soupçon of vinegar to produce an assertive small link sausage. Creole sausage is delicious on its own, as part of a gumbo, or as part of a fritto misto New Orleans style, with deep fried oysters, deep fried softshell crabs, and **rouille** sauce (see page 231) to dip everything into.*

—————— For 20 sausages, about 2½ ounces each ——— ———

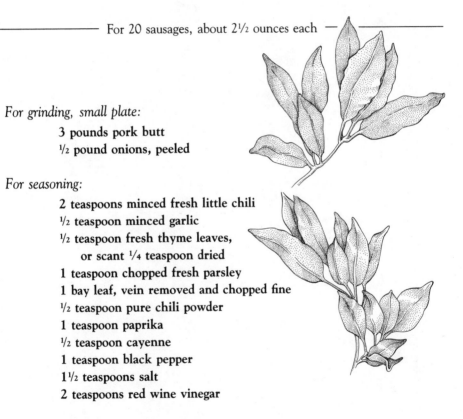

For grinding, small plate:

> **3 pounds pork butt**
> **½ pound onions, peeled**

For seasoning:

> **2 teaspoons minced fresh little chili**
> **½ teaspoon minced garlic**
> **½ teaspoon fresh thyme leaves,**
> **   or scant ¼ teaspoon dried**
> **1 teaspoon chopped fresh parsley**
> **1 bay leaf, vein removed and chopped fine**
> **½ teaspoon pure chili powder**
> **1 teaspoon paprika**
> **½ teaspoon cayenne**
> **1 teaspoon black pepper**
> **1½ teaspoons salt**
> **2 teaspoons red wine vinegar**

> **12 feet sheep casing, in 3 to 4 foot lengths, rinsed**

Mix seasonings with ground pork and onions. Stuff into sheep casing, tie at 6 inch intervals, and hang for 1 hour. Refrigerate overnight to allow flavors to blend. Will keep up to 10 days wrapped in wax or butcher paper and refrigerated.

To cook, sauté in a little butter over medium heat 10 minutes, turning to brown all around. Or parboil 5 minutes, then grill 5 minutes, or add to a composed dish for the last 10 minutes of cooking.

BOUDIN BLANC

Boudin blanc is justifiably billed as the star of French sausages. The double grinding and whipping produces a creamy, smooth texture reminiscent of the English white puddings or the veal based German bratwurst. The addition of chestnuts makes a truly stellar dish, but this presentation should be reserved for the Fall and Winter when chestnuts are fresh. It is an extra effort to peel them, but substituting canned chestnuts is expensive and ineffectual.

——————————— For 20 sausages, about 4 ounces each ———————————

For grinding, small plate:

    2 pounds boned chicken breast, including skin
    2 pounds pork butt
    1¼ pounds fatback
    ¾ pound yellow onions, peeled
    3 ounces French or Italian bread, softened in 1 cup
       heavy cream and squeezed out, cream reserved

For seasoning:

    2 large eggs
    2 teaspoons pâté spice (see page 5)
    ½ teaspoon grated nutmeg
    1 tablespoon salt

Optional:

    1½ pounds fresh chestnuts, preferably Italian, peeled
       and chopped just enough to pass through sausage
       stuffing horn without clogging
    2 tablespoons butter

    9 feet hog casing, in 3 foot lengths, rinsed; 11 feet if
       adding chestnuts

Grind ingredients once, reserving ¼ pound fatback for end of second grinding. With hands, mix together ground ingredients. Disassemble grinder and clean plate and blade; rinse with cold water. Reassemble and grind ingredients again, feeding grinder in dollops to avoid clogging. Put reserved fatback through last.

If using chestnuts, melt butter in a skillet, add chestnuts, and sauté until just beginning to turn golden. Set aside.

Add seasonings and reserved cream to stuffing. With an electric mixer, beat until the mixture is quite fluffy and sticking to sides of bowl, about 1½ minutes. If using chestnuts, add at this point and stir in without further whipping. Stuff into hog casing and tie at 4½ inch intervals. Poach 20 minutes, turning once. Remove, cool, and chill. Will keep wrapped in wax or butcher paper and refrigerated up to 1 week.

To cook, sauté in butter or grill 15 minutes, until skins are golden. Or, for a fancier preparation, peel and discard skins of poached *boudins*. Roll in fine, but not powdered, bread crumbs and sauté in butter until golden.

To peel fresh chestnuts:

With the point of a small, sharp knife, make an incision in each chestnut at the top. Drop six or seven at a time into boiling water and leave 6 minutes. Remove and cool 1 or 2 minutes. Peel skins while still quite warm. Continue with another batch.

BOUDIN NOIR

Hog's blood, the most highly esteemed for making blood sausage, is hard to find in the United States. One may settle for beef blood, which is quite as good as long as it is quite fresh. A good butcher should be able to order it for you, but don't use frozen blood: the flavor is seriously compromised by freezing and the sausages will have an unsightly blotched appearance and mushy texture. Aside from being nutritionally high in vitamins and iron, blood sausage, properly done, is a taste treat. The flavor may be varied in numerous ways: add 2 cups cooked white rice and a pinch more cayenne for a West Indian touch; make a northern French version by stirring in 2 pounds apples, peeled, cored, chopped, and wilted in 2 tablespoons butter. For an elegant brunch, serve boudins noirs with butter-creamy, soft scrambled eggs, warm French bread, and Champagne.

_____ For 18 sausages, about 4 ounces each, _____
or 4½ pounds coiled sausage

For grinding, medium plate:
> 2 pounds yellow onions
> 2 pounds fatback

For seasoning:
> ¼ cup fresh thyme leaves, or 1 tablespoon dried
> ½ heaping cup chopped fresh parsley
> 1½ teaspoons grated nutmeg
> ½ teaspoon ground allspice
> 2 tablespoons paprika
> 1 teaspoon cayenne
> 2 tablespoons black pepper
> 2 tablespoons salt

> 2 quarts very fresh blood
> ½ cup heavy cream

> 16 feet hog casing, in 2 or 3 foot lengths, rinsed

With hands, blend together onions, fat, and seasonings. Stir in blood, then add cream, which helps maintain good color.

String a length of hog casing onto the end of a large funnel. (*Boudin noir* mixture is too liquid to be fed through a machine grinder.) Tie a knot in the end of the casing and use a ladle to fill casing through the funnel, quite full if coiling sausage and not so full if tying into links. Poach 35 minutes on lowest possible heat, without allowing water to boil after sausages are added. To keep sausages immersed, cover with a lid or plate which just fits inside the pot. Remove, cool, and chill. Will keep wrapped in wax or butcher paper and refrigerated 5 days.

To cook, sauté in butter or grill 18 to 20 minutes.

BOUDIN OF CHICKEN LIVERS

Boudin of chicken livers, with the added nutty flavor of toasted walnuts, is a finer, more esoteric version of liverwurst. Serve warm with croutons and dry sherry for a festive first course before a poultry or game dinner.

—————————— For 20 sausages, about 3 ounces each ——————————

1/4 pound shelled walnuts
1 tablespoon butter or duck fat

For grinding, small plate:

1/2 pound shallots or yellow onions, peeled, roughly
    chopped, and sautéed until soft in 3 tablespoons
    butter or duck fat
2 1/2 pounds chicken livers
1 pound fatback

For seasoning:

1 tablespoon fresh thyme leaves, or 1 teaspoon dried
1/4 teaspoon grated nutmeg
2 teaspoons white pepper
1 tablespoon salt
1/4 cup brandy

2 egg whites

8 feet hog casing

Pulverize walnuts in a food processor or blender, or chop fine. In a skillet, heat butter or fat until foaming, add pulverized nuts, and stir constantly over medium heat until browned and nutty smelling. Remove from heat and set aside.

With an electric mixer or wooden spoon, mix seasonings with ground shallots or onions, chicken livers, and fat. Stir in walnuts. Beat egg whites until soft peaks form. Fold one third into boudin mixture, then stir in remainder in two batches. Fill hog casing and tie at 4 inch intervals. Poach sausages 25 minutes. Remove, cool, and chill. Will keep wrapped in wax or butcher paper and refrigerated 3 days.

To cook, sauté in butter 15 minutes, or until golden.

SWEDISH POTATO SAUSAGE

*Traditionally enjoyed on Christmas Eve, Swedish potato sausage
has an intriguing mealy texture and a simple seasoning. This
recipe was given to us by Mrs. Florence Hoffman, who serves
the sausages with a heaping pile of mashed potatoes, as the
Swedes do.*

——————————— For 20 sausages, about 4 ounces each ———————————

For grinding, small plate:

> 2 pounds beef chuck, stew, or rump
> 1 pound pork butt
> 2 pounds raw russet potatoes, peeled
> 1 medium onion, peeled

For seasoning:

> 1½ teaspoons ground allspice
> 2 teaspoons black pepper
> 1 tablespoon salt
>
> 9 feet hog casing, in 3 foot lengths, rinsed

Mix ground ingredients with seasonings. Stuff into hog casing
and tie at 4½ inch intervals. Poach 30 minutes, turning once. Remove,
cool, and chill. Will keep up to 1 week wrapped in wax or butcher paper
and refrigerated.

To serve, sauté in butter 20 minutes, until skins are golden.

SAUCISSON À L'AIL

Saucisson à l'ail *is a large cooked garlic sausage, like the French* cervelas *except that it is poached straightaway without being aged. Its hearty but not overwhelming flavor of aromatics lightly perfumed with garlic blends with many other tastes and makes it a perfect sausage for both hot and cold composed dishes.* Saucisson à l'ail *is also a good picnic sausage; just slice it and serve with a little Dijon mustard. At Christmas and New Year's, we reduce the amount of garlic slightly and add lots of roughly chopped fresh black truffle.*

————————— For 4 sausages, a bit under 1 pound each —————————

For grinding, large plate:

> **4 pounds pork butt**
> **¼ pound mild ham**
> **¼ pound fatback**

For seasoning:

> **2 tablespoons minced garlic**
> **½ teaspoon grated nutmeg**
> **1 teaspoon ground coriander seed**
> **1 teaspoon white pepper**
> **1 teaspoon black pepper**
> **¾ teaspoon cayenne**
> **1½ tablespoons salt**
>
> **4½ feet beef casing, in 1 length,**
> **or 9 feet hog casing, rinsed**

Add seasonings to ground pork and fat. Beat with an electric mixer 10 seconds, or knead vigorously with hands for 1 minute. Cover loosely and refrigerate overnight.

Next day, remove sausage from refrigerator 1 hour before stuffing. Fill casings, feeding stuffer in dollops to avoid clogging and smashing meat. Tie at 12 inch intervals. Prick each sausage once with a knife point or needle. If using beef casing, pierce on top or outside sausage, avoiding inside curve, which will burst during cooking if cut. Poach 35 minutes if using beef casing, 25 minutes if using hog casing. Turn once during cooking. Remove and serve warm, or cool and chill overnight. Will keep wrapped in wax or butcher paper up to 10 days.

COOKED TURKEY SAUSAGE

Chooch created this turkey saucisson for sausage lovers who are on a low cholesterol diet. It may be used in any of the ways suggested for **saucisson à l'ail.**

——————————— For 4 sausages, about 1 pound each ———————————

4 pounds turkey thigh meat, without skin, but including any fat

1 cup ¼-inch cubes stale white bread
1 egg
¼ cup turkey or chicken stock

For seasoning:

1 teaspoon chopped fresh sage leaves, or ½ teaspoon dried
½ teaspoon cayenne
1 teaspoon white pepper
1 teaspoon black pepper
2 teaspoons salt

4½ feet beef casing or 9 feet hog casing, in 2 lengths, rinsed

Place bread, egg, and turkey or chicken stock in a large bowl and mix a bit to coat bread. Set aside to soak.

Cut 1 pound of the turkey meat into narrow strips of any length and add to the bowl. Using small plate, grind remaining 3 pounds turkey meat and add to the bowl. Add seasoning ingredients and mix thoroughly, breaking up bread with fingers. Stuff into casing and tie at ends and middle of each length. Poach 30 minutes, turning once. Remove and serve warm, or cool and chill overnight. Will keep wrapped in wax or butcher paper up to 5 days.

BEEF SALAMI

Beef salami probably makes most people think of kosher cuisine; it makes me think of bears, since it is an adaptation of a recipe acquired on a photographing trip in Alaska. This is an easy recipe for the home cook, no special equipment or procedure being required. You may purchase ground chuck from the butcher, season it, and have your own salami in four days.

——————————— For 3 salamis, about 1½ pounds each ———————————

For grinding, small plate:

5 pounds beef chuck or stew meat

For seasoning:

4 tablespoons minced garlic
3 tablespoons mustard seed
1 tablespoon ground black pepper
1 tablespoon cracked black peppercorns
1 teaspoon saltpeter
1 teaspoon sugar
1 tablespoon salt

Mix seasonings with ground beef and knead with hands for 2 to 3 minutes. Cover and refrigerate 3 days, kneading 2 minutes once a day.

On the fourth day, remove meat from refrigerator 1 hour before continuing for easier handling. Divide into three parts. Form each third into a cylinder about 12 inches long and 2 inches in diameter. One by one, roll, pat, and work meat until sticky and all air pockets and cracks are eliminated.

To cook, place salamis at least 3 inches apart on a baking sheet in the oven. Set temperature as low as possible to maintain 160 degrees. Cook 10 hours. Remove, cool, and refrigerate. Will keep wrapped in plastic and refrigerated up to 1 month.

PRESERVED MEATS, FISH & FOWL

■ ■

T here are three ways to preserve meats, fish, and poultry: **freezing, sealing under fat,** and **curing.** All serve the same purpose of retarding decay causing bacterial action.

Freezing is the least subtle method of preserving, but it is also the most permanent: deteriorative bacterial action is completely stopped at very low temperatures, and therefore food frozen in a fresh state will remain unspoiled. However, this method is culinarily unsatisfactory since, in addition to nutritional loss, flavor and texture diminish over time.

Sealing under fat inhibits bacterial growth by excluding air and moisture. This method of preserving is usually applied to meat and poultry, although some fatty fish, such as salmon or tuna, are treated the same way to make a kind of *rillettes* sealed in and under butter. Formerly, when the preservation of meats was as much a necessity as a desire, surplus sausages often were cooked then stored under a layer of fat for longer keeping.

Food properly sealed and stored will keep 3 months or more. First, the flesh must be cooked thoroughly. Then, the layer of sealing fat must be thick enough and hard enough to keep out air and moisture. Finally, the sealed product must be stored in a place cool enough to prevent the fat from softening or melting. *Confits* and *rillettes* are examples of this kind of preserving.

Curing is a process of creating an environment hostile to bacteria by applying salt, either directly (**dry salt curing**) or in solution (**brining, pickling**). Chemically, the process is accomplished by ion hydration, which uses up water in the flesh otherwise available for microbial growth. When the salt solution is saturated, that is, 26.5 percent salt, bacterial action is halted. As a matter of taste, most brines, which include juices rendered in the dry salt curing process, are much less salty solutions, so microbial growth is inhibited but not completely stopped. In one extreme instance, **gravlax,** appealingly fresh tasting because it is so lightly and briefly cured, is by the same token barely preserved. It must be refrigerated and will keep no longer than a poached salmon.

At the other extreme, long salt curing is combined with **smoking** or **air drying.** Both of these processes preserve more thoroughly by further dehydrating the flesh. Beef jerky and many kinds of ham, which are salted for weeks, then smoked or air dried for many more weeks, are almost completely desiccated and will keep indefinitely in a cool, airy place.

Although modern refrigeration and freezing have by and large preempted the necessity for thorough preserving, we still cure meats, poultry, and fish because we enjoy the taste of cured flesh. It is hard to imagine a world without ham as long as there is cuisine.

ELEMENTS OF CURING

Salt is the major **element of curing** and the only ingredient necessary for preserving. However, salt alone produces a hardened, grayed flesh, so it is usually blended with other ingredients that counteract these unpalatable, unattractive effects. We use a fine grade powdered sea salt, available in health food stores or sometimes packaged as pickling salt, for all curing brines and most dry salt curing because it has an intense yet not harsh taste and is easily soluble. For brief, incomplete cures which do not require heavy salting, such as for *confits* and **gravlax,** we use a medium coarse sea salt, found in food specialty stores packaged as *gros sel* and usually imported from France.

Potassium or sodium nitrate, found naturally as an impurity in salt and commonly known as **saltpeter,** is an element of curing used, especially for pork, to counteract the graying effect of salt and to add an appealing rosy color. However, this can occur only after the nitrate is reduced to nitrite in the curing process. Nitrate is reduced to nitrite by the action of certain bacteria. Some recipes specify introducing a piece of meat from an old brine where these bacteria are already active into a new brine to speed up the chemical reaction and "start" the new brine.

The same purpose can be accomplished with a new brine and

fresh meat either by adding time to the curing process or by adding nitrite to the brine. A fresh brine made with saltpeter will require a minimum of 10 days to cure a leg of pork clear through, whereas a fresh brine made with nitrite will require only 6 days. The difference in potency between nitrate and nitrite can be seen in the different limits on the use of each for manufacturing set by the U.S. Department of Agriculture. Saltpeter may be used in the ratio of 4 ounces per 4 gallons of pickling brine, whereas nitrite may be mixed in the ratio of a little more than 1 ounce per 4 gallons of pickling brine.

In addition, as a source of nitrite, saltpeter serves as a botulism retardant. If you are willing to relinquish good color and some of the characteristic taste of cured meat, saltpeter may be eliminated in recipes, but care must be taken to keep the product refrigerated, even after cooking.

Curing salt is a preblended mixture of salt, sugar, and nitrite. Preblended curing salt, such as Morton's Quick Cure or Morton's Tender Cure, is sometimes available in supermarkets, although lack of demand has made it rather difficult to find. An excellent Westphalian style blend, in two pound packages—enough for many barrels of ham—is available by mail order from Carlson's Butcher Supply, 50 Mendell Street, Unit 12, San Francisco, California, 94124. If you are using a preblended curing salt with nitrite, use 1 ounce in place of the 4 ounces saltpeter in the pickling brine recipe at the end of this introduction.

Recipes in this book are written for saltpeter since it is more generally available. Most pharmacies carry nitrate, either potassium or sodium (sodium nitrate is 16 percent stronger than potassium nitrate). Saltpeter should first be dissolved in warm water, where it is more readily soluble, before mixing into the brine.

Sugar counteracts the hardening effect of salt by retaining some of the moisture which would otherwise be removed by salt. It also adds a desirable sweet flavor to the cured flesh and offsets the acidic flavor of saltpeter. Sugar does not contribute to preserving meats and fish.

Acetic acid in the form of vinegar has a mild preserving effect and is usually used in conjunction with salt. It also has a hardening effect on flesh, and we prefer not to use it except for fish, such as herring, where firming the flesh is desirable.

Aromatics, such as pepper, juniper, garlic, bay, thyme, and other herbs and spices, are elements of curing that lend flavor but do not preserve.

The recipes in this chapter are for lightly cured meats and fish, dry salted or brined, and meats and poultry preserved by long cooking followed by sealing under fat. Almost all may be easily done with no special equipment save a large crock or heavy plastic bucket and space to store it where the temperature remains between 36 and 42 degrees Fahrenheit. A meat syringe, which is a special syringe for pumping brine into the center of meat to be cured, is a handy tool for making ham and essential for pickling beef tongue, which will not cure in the center without being pumped. Meat syringes are available from butcher supply and restaurant supply stores.

A spare refrigerator where drinks are kept can be converted to storage for a pickling bucket and dry curing meats. One 5 gallon crock or bucket of pickling brine will hold, at a time, one leg of pork, one loin, one beef tongue, and several *jambonneaux*. The ambitious experimental cook may want to try all at once, removing each as it is cured and ready for further treatment. The brine should be replaced and not used again after the ham, the last out, is removed because the meats will have absorbed the salt and flavorings, leaving an ineffective, flat brine.

PICKLING BRINE:

2 pounds fine sea salt
1 pound brown sugar
4 gallons water

2 heads of garlic, unpeeled
4 bay leaves
10 sprigs fresh thyme, or 2 teaspoons dried
6 sprigs fresh sage, or 2 teaspoons dried
10 juniper berries
4 whole cloves
15 whole black peppercorns
2 cups water

4 ounces saltpeter

Wash, rinse with boiling water, and dry a 5 gallon crock, plastic bucket, or other nonreactive container. In the clean container, mix together salt, brown sugar, and water. Set aside.

In a small pot mix together remaining ingredients except saltpeter, bring to a boil, and simmer 1 minute. Stir in saltpeter to dissolve it, then add everything to brine container. Set aside overnight in the refrigerator to allow flavors to blend.

JAMBON MAISON

Jambon maison is our version of the French jambon de Paris, or jambon blanc. Found in virtually every charcuterie in France, this mildly cured, unsmoked ham is sometimes presented as a simple, squared off loaf and sometimes decorated in a fanciful way for a ham fair. We present jambon maison in a traditional American way, studded with whole cloves and glazed with mustard, honey, and sherry. Skinning and boning the leg of pork is the only task in this recipe. Have the butcher do it, or try your own hand following the instructions below.

――――――――――― For 10 to 12 pounds ham ―――――――――――

16 to 18 pound fresh leg of pork

4 gallons pickling brine (see page 104)

For the glaze:
> **1 ounce whole cloves**
> **¹/₂ cup Dijon mustard**
> **¹/₂ cup aromatic honey**
> **2 tablespoons sherry**

To prepare leg of pork, start with skin side down. Insert a curved boning knife into fat under edge of skin and work all around edge and across middle, turning leg over as necessary, to remove skin and most of fat in one piece. Set skin aside to deal with later.

With fat side down, insert knife into meat alongside pelvic bone at top of leg. Work knife down and around pelvic bone, cutting through meat, to large ball joint. Insert knife into joint to sever and remove pelvic bone. Cut through meat, moving knife alongside long leg bone. Work around leg bone to free, sever at socket, and remove bone. Don't worry if cuts are not clean; it will not be apparent in the end. Add pelvic and leg bones to meat stockpot. Trim large pieces of fat from center of

Start cut

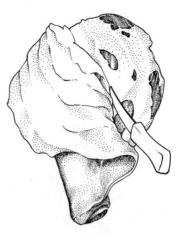

Half way, opposite side

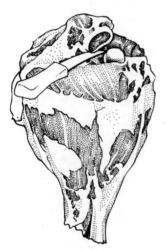

Cut at pelvic bone

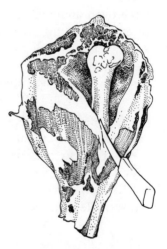

Cut leg bone free of meat

ham (about ½ pound in all) and discard. Don't completely clean off fat or ham will be too dry.

With a metal skewer, prick boned leg of pork in several places to allow brine to penetrate as meat cures. Or, use a ham syringe to pump brine into meat in several places. Drop leg into brine and cover with a scalded and cooled board or plate which will just fit into container being used. If weight is not sufficient to keep meat immersed, add another plate or so. Refrigerate or store where temperature remains between 36 and 45 degrees Fahrenheit for at least 10 days if pumped with a ham syringe or at least 14 days if pricked with a skewer. Ham may be left in the brine up to 30 days.

To cook, remove ham from brine and rinse well under cold running water. Place ham on counter and shape meat to resemble a leg of pork again. Tie in several places to maintain form. Place in a large pot and cover with cold water. Bring to a boil over high heat, then reduce heat to maintain water at a bare shudder. Cook 1 hour and 35 to 45 minutes, until an instant reading meat thermometer registers 140 degrees in center. Remove from pot and place fat side up in a roasting pan.

Preheat oven to 375 degrees. Remove all but three or four of the neatest looking strings and stud entire top of ham with cloves in a decorative pattern. In a small saucepan, heat together mustard, honey, and sherry. Stir until honey is melted, then spread mixture over ham. Place in the oven and bake 25 minutes, or until glaze is golden. Baste two or three times during cooking.

To serve, remove from oven and slice while hot, or let cool and refrigerate overnight. Will keep wrapped in plastic and refrigerated 10 days. To preserve freshness, change plastic wrap after each use.

Lard and cracklings from the skin:

Cut skin into convenient size pieces and place fat side down on baking sheets. Place in a 225 degree oven for 4 hours, until fat is rendered and skin is crispy. Pour off fat into a storage container (not plastic, which would melt). Drain skin on paper toweling. Eat cracklings, called *grattons* in French, sprinkled with salt, or crumble over potato or spinach salad.

JAMBONNEAUX

Little hams are made by curing pork forehocks in a pickling brine. They are particularly pleasing to those who like the shank of any animal for its dark meat and slightly cartilaginous texture. Cured ham hocks may be used as meat flavoring in your favorite cold weather soup, as an element in **choucroûte garnie,** *or dressed up in the manner of French charcuteries with a coating of mustard and bread crumbs to serve as a centerpiece for a picnic.*

--------------------- For 6 *jambonneaux* ---------------------

6 pork forehocks
2 gallons pickling brine (see page 104)

For the aromatic water:
> **1 cup white wine**
> **3 quarts water**
> **1 medium onion, quartered**
> **2 garlic cloves, peeled and halved**
> **2 sprigs fresh thyme, or ½ teaspoon dried**
> **1 bay leaf**
> **3 whole cloves**
> **3 allspice berries**

For the coating:
> **1 cup Dijon mustard**
> **1 cup homemade bread crumbs, not too fine**

Prepare the pickling brine. Drop in pork hocks and let them cure 5 days. They may be left in the brine up to 2 weeks.

To cook, remove hocks from brine and rinse. Place in a pot with the wine and water. Bring to a boil, skim, then add remaining ingredients for aromatic water. Reduce heat and let barely simmer 1 hour and 20 minutes.

Remove hocks and let cool 20 minutes, or refrigerate up to 5 days, before using.

To finish, preheat oven to 350 degrees. Mix mustard with bread crumbs and coat hocks with mixture. Place on a baking sheet in the oven and cook 20 minutes if still warm or 40 minutes if hocks have been refrigerated.

Serve warm for dinner accompanied with **charcuterie potatoes** (see page 138). Or refrigerate and serve cold as part of a picnic.

Jambonneaux may be used as you would smoked pork hocks. Cooked but without the mustard and breadcrumb coating, they may be added to a soup or casserole dish for the last 30 minutes of cooking time. Or they may be rinsed and added straightaway to long-cooking soups or casseroles.

CURED PORK LOIN WITH GARLIC AND APRICOTS

The surprising combination of roast pork with garlic and sun dried apricots was more familiar in Roman and medieval times when pork was often coupled with garlic and fruit. Both the color and the flavor of the pork loin benefit from a brief brining, especially if the less lean, less expensive end cut, rather than the center cut, is being used.

——————————— Dinner for 6 to 8 or a buffet platter for 20 ———————————

3 pound boneless pork loin roast, not tied
2 gallons pickling brine (see page 104)

4 ounces dried apricots, preferably sun dried
¼ cup brandy
6 garlic cloves, peeled and slivered

Immerse pork loin in brine for 24 hours, no longer or delicate meat will become too salty and hard.

To prepare apricots, soak them in brandy 20 minutes to soften. Lift loin out of brine, rinse under cold, running water, and pat dry. Place on counter, fat side down. Make an incision ½ inch deep lengthwise down center of meat. Tuck apricots in evenly along incision. Place garlic slivers on top of apricots, reserving 12 pieces for top of roast. Fold meat together, closing incision. Tie at 2 inch intervals starting in the middle and working out toward the ends. Turn fat side up and arrange reserved garlic slivers along top. Place roast fat side up in a roasting pan.

To cook, preheat oven to 475 degrees. Place pork loin in the hot oven and bake 10 minutes. Reduce heat to 350 degrees and continue baking 40 minutes, or until an instant reading meat thermometer registers 155 degrees. Cooking time will not vary much with 1 pound more or less of meat as long as diameter of tied roast is about 3 inches.

To serve hot, remove from oven, let rest 15 minutes, then slice ¼ inch thick. Accompany with a buttery purée of potato and celery root or some other root vegetable such as carrot or parsnip.

To serve cold, remove from oven, cool, cover, and refrigerate overnight. Slice thin and use as you would any cold cut. Will keep wrapped in plastic and refrigerated up to 1 week. To preserve freshness, change plastic wrap after each use.

PICKLED BEEF TONGUE

Tongue is a delicious and relatively inexpensive cut of beef. It is also quite perishable and must be cooked right away unless it is salted or dropped into a pickling brine. We prefer the pickling brine, which turns the tongue a rosy color, more appealing than the grayish brown of an uncured tongue. Unfortunately, unless brine is pumped into the center, the tongue will not be cured evenly throughout and you will wind up with brown spots here and there where the brine has not penetrated, so a ham syringe is necessary to do the recipe properly. Pickled tongue may be served warm as in recipes for fresh tongue, but is usually used as a cold cut for sandwiches or in composed salads.

_____ For a buffet platter for 25 _____
or sandwiches for a week

3 to 4 pound beef tongue
1 gallon pickling brine (see page 104)

aromatic water for cooking (see page 109)

Using a ham syringe, pump tongue in five places with pickling brine, or prick all over in 2 inch intervals with a metal skewer. Immerse tongue in pickling brine and cure 3 days if pumped, 5 days if pricked. May be left in brine up to 2 weeks.

To cook tongue, remove from brine, rinse and place in a pot with wine and water. Bring to a boil, skim, and add remaining ingredients for aromatic water. Reduce heat and simmer 2 hours. Remove and allow to cool enough to handle. While still quite warm, use a small knife and fingers to peel away thick skin and remove small bones in fatty top end. Trim off excess fat.

To serve, slice tongue crosswise as thin as possible and use for sandwiches or in a salad (see recipe for **beef tongue vinaigrette,** page 212).

PICKLED PIGS' FEET

*For quick and easy soul food, as the Bessie Smith song suggests,
"just give me a pig's foot and a bottle of beer."*

—————————————— For 1 gallon pickled pigs' feet ——————————————

6 pigs' feet without hocks, quartered

For the pickling stock:

> **2 cups white wine**
> **3 cups red wine vinegar**
> **3 quarts water**
> **⅓ pound carrots, unpeeled and quartered**
> **1 onion, unpeeled and quartered**
> **4 whole cloves**
> **1 teaspoon whole black peppercorns, cracked**
> **1 teaspoon juniper berries, bruised**
> **¼ cup fine sea salt**
> **4 bay leaves, whole**
> **4 sprigs fresh thyme, or 1 teaspoon dried**

For the aspic:

> **1 pound carrots, peeled and sliced ⅛ inch thick**
> **4 to 6 bay leaves, depending on how aromatic they are**
> **6 sprigs fresh herb: thyme, rosemary, sage, or tarragon**

Place pigs' feet, white wine, red wine vinegar, and water in a large nonreactive pot. Liquid should cover pigs' feet by 3 inches. Add more water if necessary. Bring to a boil, reduce heat to a simmer, and skim every 10 minutes for 30 minutes. Add rest of ingredients for pickling stock, partially cover, and continue simmering 2 hours. Do not let liquid boil or fat will emulsify and make stock cloudy.

With a slotted spoon or strainer carefully remove pigs' feet, discarding any stray bones. Don't worry if they seem to be falling apart at this point;

meat will firm up when chilled. Set aside to cool 1 hour. Strain hot stock into a bowl, add sliced carrots and fresh herbs, and set aside to cool and allow fat to rise to top. Discard cooked vegetables and herbs from stock.

Gently arrange cooled pigs' feet in a 1 gallon nonreactive container. A glass bowl or jar will show the dish best, but a crock or plastic bucket will do. Skim fat off stock, then fish out carrots and herbs. Tuck these into pigs' feet. Pour stock again through a strainer lined with cheesecloth or a clean dish towel over the pigs' feet. If stock has set too much to pour, reheat just enough to melt. Cover pigs' feet and refrigerate over-night before serving. Will keep refrigerated for several weeks as long as pigs' feet are covered by aspic.

Serve with mustard, *cornichons*, bread, and the bottle of beer.

PATTY'S PICKLED HERRING

It was February and the herring were running when we first tasted this excellent version of one of the most popular deli items at Patty Unterman's Hayes Street Grill in San Francisco. She generously gave us the recipe, which she had composed from different styles and methods. A higher proportion of vinegar than usual in the curing brine raises the acetic acid content, a spoilage retardant, and also firms the flesh of the fish. The sharpness is then tempered by the sugar and aromatics in the Scandinavian style flavoring brine, resulting in a dish finely balanced between sweet and sour. Ten pounds of fish may sound like a lot, but the time and effort involved in pickling herring warrant a good return for the larder. They will keep refrigerated in the brine up to 3 months, there to be pulled at a moment's notice when the hors d'oeuvre is unexpectedly up to you. Measurements may be halved or doubled as you like.

──────────── For 6 to 7 pounds pickled herring ────────────

For the curing brine:

>2 quarts water
>2 quarts white vinegar
>1¼ cups fine sea salt
>
>10 pounds very fresh herring

For the flavoring brine:

>1 pound carrots, sliced thin
>¼ pound ginger root, sliced thin
>¼ pound fresh horseradish root, peeled and sliced thin
>1 tablespoon mustard seed
>1 tablespoon whole allspice, cracked, or ½ teaspoon ground
>4 bay leaves
>3 cups white vinegar
>2 cups water
>1⅓ cups sugar

Clean a 4 gallon crock or plastic bucket with soap and water, then rinse with boiling water. In the clean container, mix together the ingredients for the curing brine. Set aside.

To clean herring, first cut off heads and discard. With a paring knife, slit bellies and thoroughly rinse fish under cool, running water. Take care to remove completely the red veins (actually the kidneys), along backbones. Place cleaned, whole fish in curing brine. To keep fish immersed, weight with a scalded board or plate just large enough to fit in the container. Refrigerate 48 hours.

Two days later, make the flavoring brine by combining all ingredients in a nonreactive pot. Bring to a boil, remove from heat, and cool. Remove herring from curing brine and rinse under cool water. Cut crosswise into 1 inch pieces. Set aside. Clean crock or bucket as above and add flavoring brine when it is quite tepid. Place fish in the brine, weight as above, and refrigerate at least 3 days before using.

To serve, lift herring and some of the vegetables out of the brine and place on a plate. Garnish with a dollop of sour cream. Better yet, make a dilled mustard cream by mixing together 1 part Dijon style mustard with 2 parts sour cream or *crème fraîche* and a sufficient amount of chopped fresh dill.

GREEN BACON

Green bacon is unsmoked bacon, somewhat like the French petit
salé, *which is saltier and generally sold already cooked, or the
Italian* pancetta, *which is a more peppery, rolled bacon. It is
a "porkier" tasting bacon than the kind usually found in American markets. To enhance the naturally sweet flavor of pork and
avoid saltiness, our green bacon is briefly cured, but not kept,
in aromatic salt without nitrate. This method produces a delicate
tasting bacon, suitable for use in any way you would use smoked
bacon or salt pork. However, it is more perishable than either
of these; after the salt is rinsed off, it will keep refrigerated 10
days and then should be stored in the freezer.*

--------------------------------- For 10 pounds bacon ---------------------------------

For the aromatic salt:

¼ **cup brown sugar**
¼ **cup black peppercorns, cracked**
1 **ounce juniper berries, crushed**
6 **bay leaves, crumbled**
1 **tablespoon fresh thyme leaves, or 1 teaspoon dried**
4 **cloves, smashed**
2 **pounds fine sea salt**

10 **pound pork belly, skin on**

Mix together ingredients for aromatic salt. Place half in the
bottom of a nonreactive container. Lay pork belly, skin side up, on top
of salt mixture. Rub remaining aromatic salt over top and sides. Or cut
pork belly to fit flat in container and place pieces on top of each other
with aromatic salt between the layers. Finish with salt on top. Cover
loosely with plastic wrap or wax paper and refrigerate for 6 days, turning
and rubbing with rendered brine daily.

After 6 days, remove bacon from salt and rinse well. Or leave 6 days more to make salt pork. Will keep refrigerated up to 10 days after salt is rinsed off, or can be frozen to preserve longer.

To cook, soak in cold water to cover for 1 to 2½ hours. Timing will depend on how long belly has been in curing salt; the best way to tell is to fry a slice and taste it after soaking 1 hour. Drain and pat dry. Will keep refrigerated up to 5 days after salt has been soaked out.

Finish cooking according to recipe being used, or slice and fry slowly over medium low heat.

LAMB HAM

Called fenalär *in Norwegian, lamb ham is also a dish of Welsh and Scottish country cuisines. While some music of the name may be lost in translation, the exotic taste remains, accentuated here by the addition of Mediterranean flavors: allspice, thyme, and lavender. Fresh lavender branch is rarely found in markets, but dried lavender or* herbes de Provence *will serve equally well to perfume the lamb in a beguiling way.*

For a 5 to 6 pound ham,
a buffet platter for 25 to 30

Lavender

8 to 9 pound leg of lamb

For the aromatic salt:

3/4 **cup fine sea salt**
2 **teaspoons saltpeter**
1/4 **cup brown sugar**
1 **tablespoon black peppercorns, cracked**
1 **tablespoon coriander seeds, cracked**
2 **tablespoons fresh thyme leaves, or 1 teaspoon dried, PLUS 1 tablespoon minced fresh lavender leaves, or 1 teaspoon dried, OR 2 teaspoons dried herbes de Provence**
1 **tablespoon whole allspice, cracked, or 1 teaspoon ground**

For the inside seasoning:

1 **tablespoon fresh thyme leaves, or 1 teaspoon dried, PLUS 1 tablespoon minced fresh lavender leaves, or 1 teaspoon dried, OR 1 teaspoon dried herbes de Provence**

120

Have butcher remove pelvic bone only from leg of lamb, or do it yourself with a curved boning knife. Leave rest of leg untrimmed at this point. Mix together ingredients for aromatic curing salt and rub all over leg of lamb. Place in a nonreactive container and refrigerate for 10 to 14 days, no longer. Turn and baste with spices and rendered juices once a day.

To prepare, wipe curing salt off lamb and place leg fat side down. Using a boning knife to make an incision through the meat next to the large leg bone. Work knife around the bone to free as neatly as possible. Insert knife in shank joint to sever and remove large leg bone. Trim away most of outside fat and the large chunk of fat from the center. Sprinkle inside with thyme and lavender leaves or *herbes de Provence.* Fold incision together and tie in several places, shaping the leg as you go.

To cook, preheat oven to 475 degrees. Place tied lamb ham in a roasting pan in the oven and roast 15 minutes. Reduce heat to 350 degrees and continue cooking 1 hour, until an instant reading meat thermometer registers 135 degrees. Remove from oven and cool. Cover and refrigerate with weight on top, such as heavy cans, overnight. Will keep wrapped and refrigerated up to 2 weeks. Change plastic wrap after each use to preserve freshness.

To serve, slice crosswise as thin as possible. Arrange on platter and garnish with watercress. Accompany with a sauce of good French mustard mixed with twice the amount of heavy cream. Or serve the Scandinavian way, with scrambled eggs and flatbread.

Preserved Meats, Fish & Fowl

CHINESE STYLE CURED PORK RIBS

In this recipe, hot red chili flakes add a Tex-Mex flair to the Chinese dish of sugar and salt cured pork, called chashiu. Chinese cooks also treat thick steaks cut from the pork shoulder, or butt, in the same way, but we prefer the tasty meat next to the bone for this somewhat sweet cure. Choose spareribs, which are fatter, rather than country style ribs, which are too lean and result in dry meat.

_____ Dinner for 6 or a buffet platter _____
or picnic dish for 10

**2 slabs pork spareribs, about 3 pounds each, backbone
joints cracked**

For the curing salt:

2 cups brown sugar
3 tablespoons soy sauce
1 tablespoon dried hot red chili flakes
2 teaspoons saltpeter
2 teaspoons fine sea salt

With a chef's knife, halve each slab of ribs down the center between 6th and 7th ribs. Mix together curing salt ingredients in a nonreactive container large enough to hold half-slabs of ribs stacked in four layers. Rub meat with curing salt mixture to coat all surfaces and place ribs in container. Cover and let cure in refrigerator 24 to 48 hours, turning pieces two or three times to baste with juices drawn out by salt.

To cook, prepare barbecue fire and let it burn to the white coal stage, or preheat oven to 350 degrees. Barbecue meat at perimeter of fire or bake in the oven 30 minutes. Turn once.

To serve, let cool enough to handle, then separate ribs with a chef's knife. Serve hot or at room temperature, sprinkled wih toasted sesame seeds. Accompany with a bowl of grated cucumber and turnip tossed with a little lemon juice, fresh coriander, and salt.

GRAVLAX

The rich and meaty Chinook (King) salmon taken from the ocean or mouth of the river produces the best textured and best tasting gravlax. More practically, a 4 pound filleted centercut from a large Silver (Coho) salmon will do nicely. Unlike the Scandinavian version, this recipe for salt and dill cured salmon uses no sugar. The salt alone will effect the cure without obscuring the flavor of the sea.

—————————— Hors d'oeuvre for 25 or a buffet platter for 35 ——————————

1 side of a 14 to 16 pound King salmon, filleted
¼ cup gros sel
2 bunches very aromatic fresh dill

To prepare salmon, turn it skin side down. Sprinkle salt over top, distributing more over thicker center part and less over thinner tail end. Slap meat with palm of hand to press in salt. Bruise dill by twisting stems and tops, then arrange over entire surface of fish. Wrap salmon in a clean cloth to absorb moisture drawn out during curing. Cover with plastic wrap.

Place salmon skin side down in refrigerator and weight with heavy cans or a board with some weight on top. Leave for 48 hours. Patted dry and rewrapped daily, gravlax will keep 7 or 8 days, but no longer as the cure is quite light.

To serve, unwrap and brush off dill and any remaining salt. Holding a knife at a 25 degree angle to the fish, slice less than ¹⁄₁₆ inch thick if possible. Arrange slices on plates or platter, garnish with a few sprigs of fresh dill, and accompany with French or brown bread, lemon wedges, and a peppermill. For very elegant cocktails, serve gravlax with a bowl of salmon roe caviar and iced aquavit or vodka.

SALMON ROE CAVIAR:

1 pound very fresh salmon roe, from a Silver or King
  salmon
2 cups boiling water
1 teaspoon sea salt

Place roe in a medium size bowl and pour the boiling water over.
Let sit 5 minutes, then add enough cool water to make temperature
tepid. With fingers, thoroughly remove outer membrane sac to release
eggs without breaking them. Let eggs fall back into water as you work.
Drain eggs in a strainer or colander, and rinse gently with cool water,
shaking off excess. Return eggs to a clean bowl and toss with salt. Store
in a glass jar with a screwtop lid in the refrigerator. Caviar will keep 10
days.

CONFIT OF GOOSE

One of the best ways of treating goose is to turn it into confit. This method of briefly salt curing, then slowly braising in fat, tenderizes the meat without drying it. Juniper, which we have added for its aromatic value to the traditional recipe, permeates the fat and meat during cooking and lends a taste both spicy and fresh. The excess fat and fatty skin of 1 goose will yield about 3 cups of rendered fat. The remaining 3 cups needed for the recipe may be rendered from other poultry or pork fat. Cutting up the goose is a bit of a struggle as the bones and joint tendons are very strong. Determination and a sharp, curved boning knife are necessary. Armed with these tools, approach the goose as though it were a tough chicken with stubbier legs; the effort is worth it. Once the bird is disjointed, little of the cook's time is required to produce a delicious, long lasting, versatile dish for the larder. Put up between Thanksgiving and Christmas when farm fresh geese are most available, the confit will be ready for a New Year's Day dish of sauerkraut and sausages, or it can be aged a bit longer to serve well in a February cassoulet. Lacking a farm fresh goose, a frozen one will do, although some of the gamy richness is lost in freezing. Lacking a goose at all, use duck with equal success, using one third the amount of seasoning or else 3 ducks. Chicken and rabbit may also be treated in the same way to make a poor man's (city slicker's) confit.

Dinner for 8 or a casserole dish for 10

8 to 10 pound goose
¼ cup, slightly rounded, gros sel
2 tablespoons fresh thyme leaves, or 2 teaspoons dried
5 bay leaves
15 juniper berries, bruised
1 tablespoon black peppercorns, cracked

6 cups rendered fat, preferably goose fat

Remove giblets, if any, from goose; set liver aside and add rest to stockpot. Trim off large pieces of fat including fatty skin pieces and neck skin flap. Place in a pan along with ¼ cup water and cook over low heat or in a 275 degree oven to render fat, about 1½ hours. Strain fat into a bowl, discarding solid pieces, and refrigerate until ready to cook *confit*.

With a boning knife, dismember goose at wing/shoulder joints, at leg/thigh joints, and at thigh/back joints. Remove breast meat from bone by inserting knife in middle at top of breast, then slicing down one side of bone and out along ribs. At top, work knife around wishbone, removing as much meat as possible. Repeat procedure for other side. Halve each breast piece crosswise. Add carcass to stockpot. Cut wings at first joint from tip end and add tips to stockpot.

Place meat, 10 pieces in all, in a nonreactive container just large enough to hold them in one layer. Spread salt, juniper berries, black pepper, thyme, and bay leaves over the top and pat into meat with your hand. Cover with plastic wrap and weight (a few heavy cans will do). Refrigerate at least 24, up to 36, hours.

To cook, preheat oven to 325 degrees, or use stovetop. Put meat along with herbs and spices into a nonreactive cooking vessel large enough to hold the pieces in one layer. In a saucepan, melt reserved rendered goose fat and whatever else you are using to make up the needed amount. Pour over goose; there should be enough almost to cover. Place in the preheated oven or on the stovetop over low heat. Cover and cook 1 hour, set cover ajar, and continue cooking another 30 minutes, or until an instant reading meat thermometer registers 200 degrees in a thigh. Remove from heat and allow to cool 30 minutes. Ladle off fat and strain into a bowl. Set fat aside to settle while meat cools enough to handle without falling apart, another 30 minutes.

To store, carefully arrange goose pieces in a clean, dry 2½ quart crockery or glass container. Crockery is best for flavor development as the *confit* ages. Strain reserved fat again and pour into the container, taking care not to include any meat juices that have settled on the bottom; add juices to stockpot. The goose must be well covered with an inch of fat to seal against spoilage. Cover and refrigerate. The *confit* is best if allowed to age at least 3 weeks; it will keep refrigerated up to 3 months providing it is completely resealed with fat each time some is used.

To serve, let *confit* stand at room temperature or in a basin of warm water until fat is softened and pieces can be easily removed. Pull out as many pieces as you want to use, scraping excess fat back into the container. If not all pieces are used at once, dig out at least 1 cup fat from confit pot, melt in a saucepan, and set aside to cool but not congeal. Chill *confit* in container. When fat is cool, pour over *confit* in container to reseal.

To serve *confit* hot, place pieces in an ungreased sauté pan. Partially cover, and cook over high heat until browned, turning once, about 15 minutes. Or use in cassoulet, in **choucroûte garnie** (see page 145), or in lentil or hearty légume soups.

To serve *confit* cold, make a salad with Belgian endive and sliced *confit*—the breast is best here—dressed with a little walnut oil and a dash of balsamic vinegar. Garnish with toasted ground walnuts, fresh coriander leaves, and freshly ground black pepper.

The goose liver:

The liver of the goose is a special treat even when it is not *foie gras*. To prepare, sauté in butter over medium high heat about 8 minutes, until medium rare. Sprinkle with salt, pepper, and ½ teaspoon of some fresh herb such as sage or thyme. Slice and eat with warm French bread.

PORK RILLETTES

A flat tire on a hot afternoon in Chablis was the occasion for a wonderful food discovery: pork rillettes and French bread with chilled Chablis. Nothing else was wanted as we waited for a kind gentleman to change the tire while we sipped the cold Chablis and parsed the mystery of rillettes, a dense, textured and yet creamy, spicy pork spread. This was a far cry from the humble beginning of the dish as cooked morsels of meat suspended in fat for preservation. For some reason, even children like rillettes. Keep a pot in the refrigerator for after school snacks.

For 3½ pounds rillettes,
a buffet dish for 25 to 30

4 pounds well marbled pork butt, boned
⅓ pound fatback or blanched salt pork
6 sprigs fresh thyme, or ½ teaspoon dried
1 bay leaf
8 garlic cloves, peeled
⅓ cup white wine
2 teaspoons salt

2 cups lard, for sealing

Cut pork and fat into strips approximately ¼ inch square and 2 inches long. Put into a heavy nonreactive pot and add remaining ingredients EXCEPT if using salt pork don't add salt yet. Cover pot, set over metal stovetop trivet, and cook over low heat 3 hours. Stir often to keep meat from sticking. Uncover pot and continue cooking 1 hour longer, stirring often. If using salt pork, taste after 1½ hours and add salt accordingly, remembering that flavor will intensify with cooking.

After 4 hours, turn contents of pot into a large mixing bowl. Include crisp parts off bottom, but leave behind any crust stuck to bottom. Fish out bay leaf and discard it. Let cool 3 hours without refrigerating, until fat is partially congealed.

To finish, heat lard until just melted and set aside. Whip rillettes with an electric beater or, more laboriously, shred with 2 forks, until meat is broken down to a stringy texture and the fat is well amalgamated. Don't overwhip or rillettes will be too creamy and the desirable stringy texture will be lost. Correct salt and pepper seasoning. Pack into a clean, dry 2 quart glass or ceramic container, pushing down as you fill to eliminate air pockets. Pour melted lard over top to seal. Refrigerate until lard is quite set, then cover with plastic wrap. Rillettes will keep refrigerated and sealed under fat up to 3 months.

To serve, scrape fat aside and scoop out as much rillettes as needed. Smooth fat back over surface to cover or remelt and pour over after cooling to reseal. Accompany rillettes with warm French bread, a peppermill, and very well chilled Chablis or other full bodied white Burgundy wine.

Or, for a large buffet or cocktail party, omit packing in a crock and sealing under lard. Instead, chill rillettes several hours, up to 5 days, to set. With hands, form into the shape of a pig. Decorate with rosemary or parsley eyelashes, olive eyes, and red pepper or pimiento lips. Tuck a flower behind her ear.

RABBIT RILLETTES

Lean meats such as rabbit do not fare well under the drying effects of freezing and long cooking. To avoid these pitfalls in making rillettes of rabbit, we use fresh rabbit and shorten the cooking time by simmering the meat in already rendered pork fat. The result is a delicate yet complex tasting spread, an unusual addition to buffet table, picnic basket, or cocktail hour.

_____ For 1 quart, about 3 pounds rillettes, _____
a buffet dish for 25

2 rabbits, about 3 pounds each
2 bay leaves
8 sprigs fresh thyme, or ½ teaspoon dried
1 head garlic, cloves peeled and halved
1 teaspoon cracked black pepper
1 teaspoon juniper berries, bruised
1½ teaspoons gros sel
½ cup gin

2 cups rendered pork fat

To prepare rabbits, remove kidneys and livers and set aside. Have butcher quarter rabbits or do it yourself with a chef's knife. Place rabbit quarters in a nonreactive container just large enough to hold pieces in one layer. Add remaining ingredients except lard, cover, and refrigerate 24 to 48 hours.

To cook, place rabbit, along with seasonings and any rendered juices, in one or two layers in a nonreactive pot. Add fat and bring to a boil over medium heat. Reduce heat to low, cover, and cook 2½ hours. Stir occasionally to keep bottom from sticking. Turn rabbit pieces over, set cover ajar, and raise heat to medium. Continue cooking 30 minutes more. Remove from heat and let cool 30 minutes.

To finish, pour fat through a strainer into a bowl and set aside. Remove rabbit meat from bones, using fingers so small splinters can be detected. Discard bones. Place meat and ½ cup reserved fat in a large bowl. Use an electric mixer or two forks to shred and mix meat just until fat is blended in and meat is still stringy. Add more fat if rillettes are too dry. Correct salt and pepper seasoning.

To store, pack rillettes into a clean, dry 1½ quart nonreactive container: crockery is best. Pour remaining unreserved fat over top to cover by ½ inch. Chill to set fat, then cover with plastic wrap. Will keep refrigerated up to 1 month sealed under fat.

To serve, push fat aside and scoop out as much rillettes as needed. Let warm to room temperature, about 45 minutes. Accompany with crunchy bread, such as croutons or Melba toasts, *cornichons,* and a peppermill.

The livers and kidneys:

In a small frying pan, melt ½ tablespoon butter plus ½ teaspoon olive or peanut oil until butter foams. Sauté kidneys over medium high heat 2 minutes, then add livers and ¼ teaspoon fresh rosemary, bay, or sage, or ⅛ teaspoon dried herb. Cook 5 to 6 minutes more, turning once, until medium rare. Remove to a plate and finish with salt and a few grinds of black pepper.

DUCK RILLETTES

The prize rillettes are those of duck meat salted and herbed overnight, simmered in its own fat, and shredded to a spreadable consistency. This is basically a method of making rillettes out of confit by longer cooking. The flavor is quintessential duck. Rendered goose, chicken, or pork fat may be used to make up the additional 2 cups needed for the final cooking if you have not managed to hoard enough duck fat for the whole amount.

——————— For about 1½ pounds, a buffet dish for 12 ———————

2 ducks

1 tablespoon fresh thyme leaves, or 1 teaspoon dried
4 bay leaves, crumbled
12 juniper berries, bruised
2 teaspoons black peppercorns, cracked
1½ tablespoons gros sel

the rendered fat from duck trimming plus 2 cups more
   rendered duck, goose, chicken, or pork fat

To prepare ducks, pull fat out of cavity and set aside in a small saucepan. Quarter ducks and trim away excess fat, adding to saucepan. Place duck in nonreactive container just large enough to fit pieces. Sprinkle remaining ingredients except fat over surface. Cover with plastic wrap, pat down to press herbs and spices into duck, and refrigerate overnight.

To render duck fat, place saucepan with fat trimming over low heat, add enough water to cover bottom of pan, and cook 2 hours until fat is melted. Remove from heat, cool, and pour through a strainer into a storage container. Refrigerate until ready to use.

To cook ducks, melt reserved rendered duck fat with additional 2 cups fat. Place duck quarters in one layer in a roasting pan or heavy pot at least 5 inches deep. Pour melted fat over duck. Fat should reach two thirds of the way up sides of duck but not cover it. Bring to a boil on the stovetop and cover with a lid or foil that fits inside the cooking container. Place in a 300 degree oven or on a metal stovetop trivet over low heat. Cook 3½ hours, turning pieces over for the last 30 minutes. Carefully remove duck to a bowl and cool 45 minutes. Strain fat into a heatproof container and set aside to cool.

To finish, remove skin and set aside. Pull meat off bones with fingers, feeling for small splinter bones as you go. Place meat in a large bowl and discard bones. Break up large pieces of duck with hands, then shred meat using an electric mixer or two forks, not a food processor. Add ¼ to ½ cup reserved cooking fat according to taste, and mix in.

To store, pack duck rillettes into a 1 quart crock or other container. Press bay leaf on top. Pour over 1 cup reserved fat to seal. Chill to set fat, cover, and refrigerate at least 2 days to blend flavors. Will keep up to 2 months sealed under fat.

The skin:

Fry duck skin in a little duck fat until crispy. Remove to paper toweling to drain, then crumble and use to garnish a salad.

MAIN
DISHES

■ ■

BOUDINS WITH POTATOES AND APPLES

Black and white sausages served with fried apples and fried or mashed potatoes is a hearty, classic French home meal.

──────────────── Dinner for 6 ────────────────

1¼ pounds boudin noir sausage (see page 89)
1½ pounds boudin blanc sausage (see page 87)
6 tablespoons unsalted butter, if sautéing sausages

¼ cup peanut oil
7 large russet potatoes, about 2½ pounds, unpeeled and
    cut into ⅛ inch dice

2 pounds good apples, unpeeled, quartered, cored, and
    sliced ¼ inch thick, lengthwise or crosswise
4 tablespoons unsalted butter
2 teaspoons fresh thyme leaves, or ½ teaspoon dried
1 tablespoon sugar

If grilling sausages, prepare the fire and let it burn until coals are white with red splotches here and there.

To cook potatoes, heat oil or shortening in a skillet until beginning to smoke. Add potatoes and stir to coat all pieces with oil. Cook, stirring frequently, over medium heat 25 minutes or until golden brown and crispy. Remove to paper toweling.

To cook apples, melt butter in a large sauté pan until foaming. Add apples, thyme, and sugar. Stir to coat all pieces with butter and cook over medium heat 20 minutes, turning once.

If sautéing sausages, melt butter in two large skillets until foaming. Place sausages on grill over coals or in skillets and cook 20 minutes, turning to brown all sides.

To serve, arrange sausages, potatoes, and apples on a large serving platter and accompany with Dijon mustard.

██ ██ ██ ██ ██ ██ ██ ██ ██ ██ ██ ██ ██ ██ ██ ██ ██ ██ ██ ██

PENNY'S HONEY GLAZED SAUSAGE

*Penny's method of honey glazing and baking fresh sausage is
particularly suitable for saucisse Polonaise or Toulouse sausage.
Served with her favorite charcuterie potatoes, honey-glazed sausage makes a satisfying, simple meal.*

――――――― Dinner for 6 ―――――――

2 to 2½ pounds saucisse Polonaise (see page 83) or
    Toulouse sausages (see page 78)
½ cup light, aromatic honey

Preheat oven to 350 degrees. Parboil sausages 10 minutes. Remove to baking sheet and cool 20 minutes. Coat with honey and bake
30 minutes, basting every 10 minutes. Serve with charcuterie potatoes.

CHARCUTERIE POTATOES:

3 pounds russet potatoes, peeled and cut into ⅛ inch
    thick rounds
¼ pound butter
salt
freshly ground black pepper
1½ to 2 cups heavy cream

Preheat oven to 350 degrees. Arrange potato slices in layers in a
baking pan, dotting with butter and sprinkling with salt and pepper as
you go. Pour in cream, enough to come two thirds of the way up sides
of the potatoes. Bake 1 hour, until cream bubbles up over top and top
is golden.

CHOOCH'S PITTSBURGH SAUSAGE

This is Chef Chooch's favorite way to prepare his sweet Italian sausage.

──────── Lunch or dinner for 6 ────────

For the sauce:

⅓ cup olive oil

2 medium yellow onions, peeled and cut lengthwise into
   ½ inch strips

3 green bell peppers, halved, seeded, and cut lengthwise
   into ½ inch strips

2 large garlic cloves, peeled and minced

2 little hot red or green chilies, minced, or ½ teaspoon
   dried red chili flakes

2 tablespoons fresh oregano leaves, or 1½ teaspoons dried

2 pounds fresh, ripe tomatoes, chopped and juices
   reserved, or 3 cups canned Italian plum tomatoes,
   drained and chopped, juices reserved

salt

freshly ground black pepper

1½ to 2 pounds sweet Italian sausages (see page 79)
1½ tablespoons olive oil

To make the sauce, heat ⅓ cup olive oil in a large nonreactive skillet. Add onions, peppers, garlic, oregano, and chilies. Sauté over moderate heat about 5 minutes until onions and peppers have softened but not browned. Add tomatoes with reserved juices. Reduce heat and simmer uncovered for 1 hour. Taste sauce and add salt and pepper.

To finish, sauté sausages in 1½ tablespoons olive oil 10 minutes, turning to brown all around. Add to sauce and simmer 20 minutes.

To serve, place sausage on French or Italian bread and spoon sauce over. Or accompany with pasta tossed with garlic, olive oil, Parmesan cheese, and plenty of fresh basil. Or serve with polenta fried in softened butter mixed with an equal amount of good feta cheese.

SUSANNA'S PIGS IN BLANKETS

Our friend Susanna, an inspired cook who has contributed many recipes and ideas to our repertoire over the years, created this dish as a showcase for our Champagne sausages. The preparation calls for rapid braising to seal in juices and frequent basting to deepen color and taste. The resulting succulent and pretty dish is quick and easy, a trick worthy of any cook's bag. Follow the recipe for Champagne sausage in the sausage chapter, or substitute a ready-made small link sausage which is not so spicy that it overwhelms the subtlety of the tarragon. Sliced leftover pigs in blankets are a lovely addition to any charcuterie platter.

--- Dinner for 6 ---

3 tablespoons butter
6 Champagne sausages (see page 84)
3 whole chicken breasts, boned
¼ teaspoon black pepper
8 garlic cloves, minced
3 cups red or rosé wine
1 tablespoon fresh tarragon leaves, or ½ teaspoon dried

Melt butter in a nonreactive skillet. Over moderate heat, sauté Champagne sausages in butter 5 minutes to brown lightly. Remove from heat and set aside.

Halve chicken breasts lengthwise and flatten each half with palm of hand. Wrap each sausage in a half breast, using toothpicks to secure.

Return skillet to medium high heat; add chicken breasts and black pepper. Sauté 6 or 7 minutes, turning several times to brown all around. Add garlic and sauté 1 minute more. Add wine and tarragon, reduce heat, and cook 10 minutes longer, basting frequently. Remove chicken rolls to a hot platter. Reduce liquid in pan over high heat until bubbles break from bottom rather than just from the surface. Pour over pigs in blankets and serve with a bowl of saffron rice.

CABBAGE TURBAN

Largely helped by good press about the nutritional value of all the cabbages, including broccoli, cauliflower, brussels sprouts, and bok choy, cabbage dishes enjoy more popularity now than they did ten years ago. For those still prejudiced against this homely vegetable, cabbage turban, made with sweet and tender little cabbages, should be irresistible. The best version of the dish is made in the late Spring with young cabbage of not more than 2 pounds. Fresh Roma or saladette tomatoes suitable for cooking should be available by then.

Dinner for 4

For the aromatic water:
> 2 whole cloves
> 2 bay leaves
> 1 tablespoon salt
> 3 quarts water

> 1½ pounds green cabbage
> 1⅓ pounds crépinettes (see page 77) or sweet Italian
>   sausage (see page 79), not in casing

Place ingredients for aromatic water in a large pot and bring to a boil. Add whole cabbage, reduce heat, and simmer 10 minutes. Lift cabbage out and drain in a colander until cool enough to handle, about 20 minutes. Reserve aromatic water.

Without severing them from the core, separate cabbage leaves one by one down to hard center core leaves. Cut or twist off core and set aside. Place one quarter of sausage stuffing in center of cabbage and fold up first layer of leaves to cover. Spread more stuffing around outside of first layer, fold up next layer of leaves, and continue to the outside, patting cabbage into shape as you go.

Wrap the stuffed cabbage in a length of cheesecloth, twisting and tying ends together with string to form a compact unit. The cabbage turban may be refrigerated as is up to 2 days; add 10 minutes to cooking time if refrigerated.

To cook, bring reserved aromatic water to a boil, lower cabbage in, reduce heat to maintain simmer, cover, and cook 45 minutes, or until an instant reading meat thermometer registers 145 degrees. Remove cabbage to a colander and let drain 10 minutes before unwrapping.

To serve, remove cheesecloth and cut cabbage turban into wedges. Accompany with fresh tomato and caper sauce and boiled parslied potatoes.

TOMATO AND CAPER SAUCE:

3/4 cup olive oil
1 1/2 pounds fresh ripe tomatoes, peeled, seeded, and cut
    into 1/4 inch dice
grated rind of 1 lemon
3 ounces capers, preferably large, rinsed and squeezed
    dry
3 large garlic cloves, peeled and roughly chopped
salt
1/4 cup heavy cream (optional)

Heat oil in a large nonreactive skillet. Add tomatoes and stir. Add lemon rind, capers, and garlic and stir. Cook just to the boiling point, then remove from heat. Add salt to taste. If you feel like gilding the lily, stir in the cream. The sauce will keep refrigerated up to 10 days if cream has not been added. Tomato and caper sauce is also good with fish such as halibut, tuna, or Spanish mackerel.

BREAST OF VEAL NIÇOISE

Cookbook writers like to point out that stuffed breast of veal is good tasting, eye appealing, and economical. Its lack of popularity among home cooks must be due to its somewhat indecipherable bony form. In this recipe, a pocket is slit open, filled with the stuffing, and sewn up with no further fussing. As the dish simmers, the bones add a depth of flavor especially pronounced if the veal breast is stored overnight in the poaching liquid and served cold the next day.

——————————— Dinner for 8 or a picnic ———————————
or buffet dish for 15

1 veal breast, about 3½ pounds

For the stuffing:

1 pound fresh spinach

2½ pounds sweet Italian sausage (see page 79), not in casing

½ cup pitted Niçoise olives or ¼ cup pitted oil-cured black olives

2 tablespoons olive oil

2 tablespoons butter

For the poaching liquid:

1 small carrot, unpeeled and cut into 1 inch pieces

2 stalks celery, cut in 1 inch pieces

1 small onion, unpeeled and quartered

2 sprigs fresh thyme, or ¼ teaspoon dried

1 quart dry white wine

2 cups water

Have butcher open a pocket in the veal breast, or do it yourself with a curved boning knife. Starting at large end, insert blade 5 inches into layer of fat between meat and bone. Slit along bones to make opening almost, but not quite, to other end.

To make stuffing, cut spinach leaves crosswise into 1/2 inch thick strips and chop stems. Immerse in plenty of cold water, let sit a few seconds so dirt will settle to bottom, then lift out. Repeat with fresh water, then lift out into a colander to drain again. Place wet spinach in a nonreactive pot and stir over medium heat until wilted. Drain and cool. Squeeze out excess liquid and add spinach to sausage and olives. Mix with hands.

To assemble and cook, pack stuffing into the pocket in the veal breast. Close opening and secure with skewers or sew with needle and thread. Melt oil and butter in a large nonreactive roasting pan deep enough to hold veal breast and liquid. Brown veal breast over medium high heat 10 minutes on each side. Add ingredients for poaching liquid and bring to a boil. Reduce heat to maintain liquid at a simmer. Cover with foil, pinch around edges to seal, and cook on stovetop or in a 350 degree oven 2 hours.

Remove from heat, uncover, and let veal breast cool in the poaching liquid 15 minutes if serving warm. If serving cold, cool completely, cover, and refrigerate in the poaching liquid overnight or up to 5 days.

To serve, carve into chops, cutting between rib bones, or neatly remove bones first, then cut into 1/4 inch thick slices. Accompany with Dijon mustard and warm French bread.

Note: If serving cold, a tasty aspic garnish may be made from the poaching liquid. Remove any fat from liquid when cold. Heat liquid just to melting, then pour through a strainer lined with clean cloth into a clean, nonreactive pot. Remove 1/2 cup liquid to a small bowl and set aside. Bring the liquid in the pot to a boil. Dissolve 1 tablespoon unflavored gelatin in the reserved liquid in the bowl, and whisk into boiling liquid. Remove from heat immediately, strain through a clean cloth into a rectangular container, and chill until set. Cut into squares, diamonds, or any other shape and use to decorate the veal breast.

CHOUCROÛTE GARNIE

Choucroûte garnie *is cabbage in its most elegant manifestation,*
patiently fermented into sauerkraut, braised with ham hocks
(jambonneaux), juniper, and white wine, and served up gar-
nished with preserved poultry and fresh sausage. This dish of
humble bounty is elevated to the realm of divine satisfaction
when the elements are homemade, but a very respectable feast
can be concocted from purchased ingredients. The quality of
commercial sauerkraut varies enormously: choose a variety, bulk
or jarred, which is not too finely shredded, as this tends to be
soft and not fresh tasting. The ham hocks, preferably fresh and
not smoked, are essential, and it is not too much trouble to drop
a few into a pickling brine 5 days before assembling the chou-
croûte. Smoked ham hocks from the butcher may be substituted
in a pinch. There is no substitute for confit of duck or goose,
but fresh roasted duck, goose, or pork loin all make a fine garnish
for sauerkraut. Sausage possibilities are numerous; if you are
not making your own, buy good quality kielbasa or fresh sausage
from a French or German deli. After the quality of the ingre-
dients, the next most important element in producing excellent
choucroûte garnie *is the cooking vessel. An ovenproof unglazed*
terra cotta container, such as a Romertopf, which mysteriously
both seals in juices and allows steam evaporation, makes all the
difference in the final taste of the dish. Glazed terra cotta or
heavy duty enamelware such as Copco or Creuset are second
choices. In any case, the pot must be of nonreactive material to
avoid having a metallic taste permeate the whole dish and over-
whelm the sweet/acid balance between meats and sauerkraut.

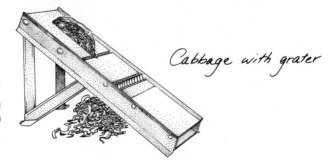

Cabbage with grater

For cooking the sauerkraut:

3 pounds fresh sauerkraut (recipe follows)

3 tablespoons duck fat, goose fat, or butter

1/4 pound bacon (see page 16), pancetta, or blanched
    salt pork, cut into 1 inch squares 1/2 inch thick

3 medium yellow or white onions, about 1 pound,
    peeled and cut into 1/4 inch thick slices

3 sprigs fresh thyme

1 bay leaf

1 teaspoon black peppercorns, cracked

10 juniper berries, crushed

3 to 5 large garlic cloves, peeled and halved

2 jambonneaux (see page 109), uncooked

1 cup light beef or pork stock

2 cups white wine—Riesling, dry Gewurztraminer, or
    Chablis

confit of 1 duck or 1/2 goose (see page 125)

1 pound saucisson à l'ail, saucisse Polonaise or Tou-
    louse sausages (see pages 94, 83, 78)

1 1/2 tablespoons duck fat, goose fat, or butter

Place sauerkraut in a colander and rinse more or less thoroughly depending on degree of saltiness. Do not wash out all the brine or dish will be bland. Lightly press out excess liquid without completely drying the sauerkraut and set aside. In a large nonreactive skillet, melt fat or butter. Add bacon, pancetta, or blanched salt pork and cook over medium low heat 5 minutes without browning. Add onions, stirring and turning to coat all pieces with fat. Cook 20 minutes, stirring occasionally, until onions are wilted but not browned. Remove ingredients to a 3 quart Romertopf or other heavy, nonreactive ovenproof pot.

Add sauerkraut to onions in the oven pot, separating strands with two forks and stirring about to mix well and coat with fat. Tie herbs, spices, and garlic in cheesecloth and bury in sauerkraut. Bury *jambonneaux* or ham hocks in sauerkraut. Add stock and white wine. Cover pot, place in the oven and set heat at 375 degrees if using Romertopf, 325 degrees otherwise. Cook undisturbed 2 hours.

When sauerkraut has cooked for 2 hours, uncover, turn top layer under, and add a little water if liquid has evaporated below two thirds full level. Add pieces of duck or goose *confit*, reduce oven heat to 300 degrees, replace cover, and continue cooking 30 minutes.

If using *saucisson à l'ail*, cut into 2 inch pieces. If using Polonaise or Toulouse sausages, parboil 10 minutes. Ten minutes before sauerkraut is cooked, brown sausage in fat or butter until cooked through. Remove to paper toweling.

To serve, lift cheesecloth bag out of choucroûte and discard it. Turn the mixture over once, then arrange meats on top of sauerkraut in the cooking pot or on a large platter. Accompany with boiled, parslied potatoes and ice cold beer.

SAUERKRAUT:

Choose large, mature heads of green cabbage. Small heads will not have developed enough sugar for full flavor and will not render enough water when salted to make brine sufficient to cover cabbage. Cabbage must remain below brine level or it will spoil rather than ferment.

25 pounds Savoy, Napa (Chinese), or other green cabbage
1 1/4 cups coarse salt or gros sel

First, clean a 4 gallon crock or plastic container and a plate or board just large enough to fit inside container by washing with warm, soapy water and rinsing with boiling water. Set aside.

If using Savoy or close-headed green cabbages, remove and discard damaged outer leaves. Rinse and quarter cabbages. Hold cabbage quarter by core and, using a mandoline, cut into strands 1/8 inch thick and as long as possible. Or remove cores and, using a chef's knife, cut quarters lengthwise into 1/8 inch thick shreds. If using Napa cabbage, rinse and shred whole cabbages with a chef's knife, cutting into 1/8 inch thick shreds crosswise.

Pack shredded cabbage into the clean container in layers, salting and tamping down hard on each layer with a pestle, wooden mallet, or small

147

cutting board as you go. Water will begin to be released. When all cabbage is salted and packed in, mound top slightly so weight will be distributed over entire surface. Cover with a clean cloth rinsed in cold water and wrung not quite dry. Place the scalded plate or board on top of cloth and weight with a scalded brick, rock, or quart jar scalded on the outside and filled with water.

Check the liquid level after 2 hours. If not enough liquid has been released to cover cabbage completely, make a brine by boiling 4 cups water with 1½ tablespoons sea salt. Cool to tepid. Remove weight, plate or board, and cloth from container, pour in enough brine to immerse cabbage completely, and replace cloth, plate or board, and weight.

Store container in 65 to 75 degree room out of sunlight. Leave 10 days, then remove weight, plate or board, and cloth. Clean and scald weight and plate or board and set aside to cool. Rinse cloth well with cool water and wring not quite dry. Set aside. With scalded spoon or ladle, skim off any scum and wipe sides of container with a clean damp cloth. Replace cloth, plate or board, and weight. Restore container. Repeat process every 5 days.

Cabbage is turned into sauerkraut in 3 to 5 weeks, depending on room temperature. The warmer the room, the less time it takes to complete the cure. Fermentation is complete when brine no longer bubbles. When cured, store sauerkraut in refrigerator. Will keep refrigerated up to 1 month. For longer keeping, pack into sterilized jars and process, preferably in a pressure canner.

■ ■

VERONICA'S TWO DAY GUMBO

This is Veronica's version of her mother's Charleston style okra soup, which included no shrimps or sausage but added corn and lima beans. Vary the ingredients as you like without compromising the basic components: a rich pork broth with okra, smoked ham hock, and chicken marinated with garlic. Canned tomatoes and dried thyme, rather than fresh, are essential to produce the characteristic deep and musty flavor of this dish from a cuisine built around stored and preserved goods. Frozen okra may be used if fresh is not available, in which case it is easiest to cut the okra while it is still partially frozen—defrosted okra is slippery and hard to hold on to. The recipe is generous enough to allow some leftovers as gumbo is delicious up to a week later. Remove any shrimps or oysters remaining after the first serving; they will ammoniate and spoil the broth. If using corn, cut the kernels off the cob and add 5 minutes before finishing. If using lima beans, add when okra is added.

―――――――――――――――― Dinner for 6 and some leftovers ――――――――――――

For the broth:

> 8 pounds pork bones, including, if possible, a prosciutto
>   bone first blanched 15 minutes
> 1 jambonneau (see page 109), 1 to 1½ pounds, uncooked
> 2 medium yellow onions, unpeeled and quartered
> 6 sprigs fresh parsley
> 1 teaspoon dried thyme
> 2 bay leaves
> 8 quarts water
>
> 2 tablespoons olive oil
> 2 medium yellow onions, peeled and cut into ¼ inch
>   dice
> 2 stalks celery, cut into ¼ inch dice
> 2 medium green bell peppers, cut into ¼ inch dice
> 1 teaspoon dried thyme

3 28-ounce cans Italian plum tomatoes, including juices
    of 2 cans
1 smoked ham hock
½ teaspoon cayenne

6 chicken wings
10 garlic cloves, crushed

1½ pounds okra, cut in ¼ inch rounds
1½ tablespoons light olive or peanut oil
1 pound saucisson á l'ail (see page 94), cut in 1 inch
    thick pieces
1 pound headless, medium size shrimps
12 to 16 fresh oysters, shucked, juices reserved

First day, place ingredients for broth in a large nonreactive pot, or divide evenly between two pots. Bring to a boil, reduce heat to maintain a simmer, cover, and cook 2½ hours. Pour stock through a strainer lined with clean cloth into a storage container. Remove and discard bones from *jambonneau*, roughly chop meat, and add to the strained broth. Let cool to room temperature, then refrigerate overnight.

Sever chicken wings at "elbow" joints, place in a bowl, and toss with crushed garlic and a little salt and freshly ground black pepper. Cover and refrigerate overnight.

Next day, heat olive oil in a skillet. Add onions, bell pepper, celery, and thyme. Cook over medium heat until vegetables are wilted. Skim and discard fat off the top of the prepared stock. Place the stock in a nonreactive pot and add wilted vegetables. Add tomatoes, breaking up slightly with hands but not chopping. Add tomato juices, ham hock, and cayenne to the pot and place on medium heat. Bring to a boil, reduce heat, and simmer 2½ hours.

To finish, add cut okra to the pot and continue simmering. Heat oil and brown chicken wings with garlic 5 minutes. Add to the pot and cook 25 minutes. Twenty minutes after adding chicken, stir in shrimps and sausage. Continue simmering 5 minutes. At last minute, add oysters and oyster juices. Remove pot from heat and serve immediately. Accompany with polenta or cornbread.

POSOLE

Like Basque garbure, Italian minestrone, or American chile Colorado, posole is a variation on the theme of stalwart pork and vegetable soups. It takes its name from the dried corn used in place of the more usual dried beans. Dried or wet pack corn is hard to find outside New Mexico, but is worth mail ordering (see note). Canned hominy is a poor substitute for this delicious cereal which, along with the dried hot chilies, gives the soup its characteristic, slightly musty, Southwestern and Mexican flavor. Some cooks include tomatoes; others don't. Most recipes call for pork shoulder (pork butt) meat, but we prefer the tasty and succulent meat next to the rib bones, which holds up better during long cooking. Have the butcher cut across the slab of ribs with his electric saw. At home, cut between ribs to separate into small pieces.

──────────────── Dinner for 6 ────────────────

2 cups dry posole
water

2 tablespoons vegetable oil
2 ounces pork rind, from bacon or blanched salt pork,
    cut into bite size pieces
2 pounds pork spareribs, cut crosswise into thirds, then
    ribs separarated

1 fresh pig's foot, quartered
3 pounds pork bones
4 quarts water

1 pound fresh tomatoes, peeled, seeded, and chopped, or
    2 cups canned Italian plum tomatoes, chopped,
    juices strained and reserved
2 whole garlic cloves, peeled
1 whole medium onion, peeled
1 tablespoon chopped fresh oregano leaves, or 1 tea-
    spoon dried
½ teaspoon salt

For the chili sauce:

> 4 large dried red chilies
> 2 garlic cloves, peeled and halved
> 1 teaspoon pure chili powder
> 1½ cups water
> ½ teaspoon salt

For the garnishes:

> 2 cups finely diced avocado
> ¼ cup chopped fresh oregano leaves, or 2 tablespoons
>   dried
> 6 lime wedges

Place posole in a medium size pot, add water to cover by 3 inches, and bring to a boil. Remove from heat and let soak 1 hour. Drain and rinse, return to pot with fresh water to cover by 3 inches, and bring to a boil. Simmer 1 hour and 45 minutes, or until kernels have popped open. Remove from heat and set aside. Posole may be prepared up to 2 days in advance, cooled to room temperature, and refrigerated in the cooking liquid.

Heat oil in a skillet. Brown pork rind 5 minutes, then remove to an 8 quart nonreactive pot. Add pork spareribs to skillet and brown 5 minutes. Transfer to pot with rind. Add posole and its liquid, pig's foot quarters, pork bones, and water. Bring to a boil, reduce heat to maintain a simmer, and skim. Cook 30 minutes then skim again, removing as much fat off the top as possible. Add tomatoes along with their strained juices, garlic, onion, and oregano. Partially cover and cook at the barest simmer 2 hours. Fish out pig's foot pieces and pork bones. Remove bones from pig's foot pieces and discard, along with pork bones. Slice skin into thin strips and return to pot along with meat. Continue cooking 1 hour.

To prepare chili sauce, halve chili pods and remove stems and seeds. Place in a small saucepan along with garlic, chili powder, and 1½ cups water. Bring to a boil, then simmer 15 minutes, or until chilies are tender and garlic is cooked through. Cool 15 minutes, then purée in a blender or food processor. Or strain the liquid into a bowl and reserve it. With a wooden mallet or in a mortar, pound garlic and chilies to a purée, gently so it does not splash all over, then stir into the strained liquid in the bowl. Stir in salt. Set chili sauce aside.

When soup has cooked 3 hours, remove and discard onion. Add 3 tablespoons chili sauce and simmer 30 minutes more.

To serve, ladle posole into large bowls and accompany with garnishes on the side, warm tortillas, butter, and remaining chili sauce.

Note: Posole in 1 pound packages may be mail ordered from Bueno Foods, 2001 Fourth St., SW, Albuquerque, New Mexico, 87102, 505-243-2722.

ARAYAH'S CHILE COLORADO

Arayah's chile Colorado is actually Texas style red chili without the beef or cumin. With tongue in cheek, we call it charcuterie Californienne and, adding whim to fantasy, serve it with a Creole flair, alongside white Italian rice sprinkled with fresh thyme. Chile Colorado requires long, slow cooking, and is best if ingredients are prepared and assembled, then cooked two hours one day and finished the next. Cool completely before refrigerating overnight.

_____ For 3 quarts chili, dinner for 8 or a buffet _____
dish for 12

For the kidney beans:

>   3 cups dried red kidney beans
>   1 bay leaf
>   2 teaspoons salt
>   1 tablespoon red wine vinegar
>   water
>
>   2 large dried red chilies
>   2 cups water

For the meat:

>   5 pounds pork butt
>   1 teaspoon olive or peanut oil
> $1/2$ teaspoon chili powder
> $1/4$ teaspoon cayenne

For the vegetables:

> $1/4$ cup olive or peanut oil
>   2 pounds yellow onions, cut into $1/2$ inch dice
>   1 pound green bell peppers, cut into $1/2$ inch dice
>   2 ounces garlic, peeled and roughly chopped
>   1 tablespoon fresh oregano leaves, or 1 teaspoon dried
>   1 teaspoon red chili flakes
> $1/2$ teaspoon cayenne

½ teaspoon black pepper
1½ teaspoons salt

5 pounds fresh Roma, or canned Italian plum, tomatoes,
    cut into ¼ inch dice
juice of the tomatoes
1 tablespoon tomato paste
3 cups pork stock or water

To prepare kidney beans, place in a large pot and cover with water by 3 inches. Bring to a boil, remove from heat, and set aside to soak 1 hour.

Remove stems and seeds from large dried chilies and place chilies in a pot with 2 cups water. Bring to a boil, then simmer 30 minutes to soften chilies. Remove chilies and halve them, then quarter each half. Set aside until ready to sauté meat. Reserve chili water.

When beans have soaked 1 hour, drain in a colander and rinse under cold water. Return to the pot, along with bay leaf, salt, vinegar, the reserved chili water, and enough more water to cover by 3 inches. Bring to a boil, reduce heat just to maintain a simmer, and cook 1 hour, or until beans are quite done. Drain and set aside.

To prepare meat, trim fat off outside of pork butt and reserve for another use. Cut pork into ½ inch cubes, trimming away any large pieces of fat. Heat oil in a large skillet and, in several batches, sauté meat with chili powder, cayenne, and softened dried chilies until meat is well browned. Remove to an 8 quart nonreactive pot.

To prepare vegetables, heat oil in a skillet and sauté onions, green bell peppers, garlic, oregano, red chili flakes, cayenne, black pepper, and salt until onions and peppers are wilted. Transfer to the pot with the meat.

Add tomatoes along with juices, tomato paste, kidney beans, and pork stock or water to pot with pork and vegetables. Bring to a boil, reduce heat, and cook at barest simmer 4½ hours, or until liquid is quite thick. Stir occasionally.

Serve as suggested, or with corn bread or tortillas, or polenta. Accompany with a bowl of steamed fresh vegetables dressed with olive oil and chopped fresh garlic. Chili will keep covered and refrigerated up to 1 week, or up to 2 weeks if heated to boiling every 4 days.

LISA'S GREEN CHILI

Lisa's New Mexico version of chile verde is an excellent re-
frigerator dish, which can happily be reheated all week. The
bother of roasting and peeling fresh Anaheim chilies is worth it
for the special taste they impart to the dish. Tinned peeled green
chilies will also do nicely.

—————————————— Dinner for 6 or a buffet dish for 10 ——————————————

6 pounds pork butt, bone in
1 tablespoon peanut oil
salt
black pepper

2 medium onions, peeled and cut into ¼ inch dice
8 garlic cloves, peeled and roughly chopped
2 little hot green chilies, minced
1 tablespoon fresh oregano leaves, or 1 teaspoon dried
1 teaspoon salt

1½ pounds fresh long green (Anaheim) chilies, or 3
    4-ounce cans peeled whole green chilies

2 cups light beef or pork stock
2 quarts water

Remove bone from pork butt and set aside. Trim fat off outside
of pork and cut into ¼ inch dice. Heat oil in a large skillet, add diced
fat, and cook over low heat 30 minutes to render.

Cut pork butt across the grain into ¼ inch thick steaks. Cut each
steak into long strips ¼ inch wide, trimming away any large pieces of
fat as you go. Add fat trim to skillet with rendering lard. Set pork meat
aside.

After 30 minutes, remove cracklings from lard skillet to paper toweling and set aside. Pour off all but 3 tablespoons lard from skillet into

a storage container and reserve for other uses. Preheat oven to 475 degrees if using fresh Anaheim chilies.

Heat lard in the skillet and add onions, garlic, little green chilies, oregano, and salt. Sauté until onions are wilted. Remove to a heavy pot.

In the same skillet, stir fry pork in several batches until pale in color, seasoning each batch with a little salt and black pepper. Add meat to vegetables in pot as you go.

When pork is sautéed, turn up heat under skillet and deglaze with ¼ cup water, scraping up brown bits on bottom. Add to pot along with remaining water, the stock, and reserved bone. Bring to a boil, skim, then reduce heat to maintain the barest simmer. Cook over low heat while preparing Anaheim chili peppers.

If using fresh chili peppers, place in a hot oven 20 to 25 minutes, until they are charred all around and skin is crackled. Or place over gas flame and turn to char all around, about 6 to 8 minutes. Place charred chilies in a large brown paper bag and close bag. Let sit 5 minutes to steam, then peel off skins. Remove and discard seeds and cores from fresh or canned chili peppers, then cut into long strips ¼ inch wide. Add to pot with meat, stir to mix in, partially cover, and cook at the barest simmer 2½ hours. Stir occasionally.

To serve, ladle into bowls and accompany with sliced fresh tomatoes sprinkled with a little red wine vinegar and crumbled cracklings, hot buttered tortillas, and ice cold Mexican beer.

157

JUDITH'S PORK CHOPS WITH CARROTS AND CARDAMOM

Wine merchant and friend Judith Shane has provided us with many a delightful culinary surprise. In this dish, ground cardamom adds an exotic flavor of Indian cookery, which uses spices rather than herbs as the major seasoning. Purchase the less expensive pork chops from the end of the loin; centercut chops are too lean and will dry out during the long cooking.

--- Dinner for 6 ---

6 pork chops, less than ½ inch thick and not too lean
salt
freshly ground black pepper

1 onion, peeled and cut into ½ inch dice
12 garlic cloves, peeled and roughly chopped
3 tablespoons peanut oil
2 tablespoons unsalted butter

For the sauce:

2 pounds fresh tomatoes, peeled, seeded, and chopped,
    or 2 cups canned Italian plum tomatoes, drained
    and chopped
juices of the tomatoes
2 tablespoons rich tomato paste
1 cup chicken stock
½ cup white wine
2 bay leaves
3 inch cinnamon stick
½ teaspoon ground cardamom
⅛ teaspoon freshly grated nutmeg
½ teaspoon salt
plenty of freshly ground black pepper

2 pounds carrots, peeled and cut into ½ inch thick
   rounds
2 tablespoons unsalted butter
water

2 tablespoons chopped fresh parsley or coriander

Trim excess fat from outside of pork chops and sprinkle each side with salt and pepper. Set aside. In a large nonreactive skillet, sauté onion and garlic in peanut oil until wilted but not browned. Remove to a plate and set aside. In the same skillet, melt butter and brown pork chops on both sides, about 5 minutes. Return onion and garlic to skillet along with sauce ingredients. Stir to mix ingredients, cover, and cook over medium low heat 2 hours.

Place carrots and butter in a nonreactive saucepan along with enough water to cover barely. Bring to a boil, reduce heat to medium, and cook uncovered 15 minutes. Turn heat up to brown slightly 5 minutes, then remove from heat and set aside in a warm spot.

After pork chops have cooked 2 hours, ladle 1 cup sauce out of skillet into the bowl of a food processor or blender. Add 1 cup cooked carrots and process or blend to purée. Or push through a strainer or food mill to purée. Set aside.

To serve, arrange pork chops on a platter and strew cooked carrots over top. Set platter aside in a warm spot. Mix purée into the sauce in the skillet, heat to boiling, then pour over pork chops and carrots. Sprinkle with chopped fresh parsley or coriander and accompany with steamed rice.

DALI POTATOES

Quid pro quo, *we named our rillettes-stuffed potatoes after Salvador Dali's recipe for charcuterie potatoes, of which they are a homely variation. Who knows, he may have got the idea, and embellished it, from Jane Grigson, who mentions the French habit of eating grillons with mashed potatoes.*

——————————————— Dinner for 6 or a side dish for 6 ———————————————

6 large russet potatoes

1 pound pork rillettes (see page 128), at room temperature
6 tablespoons heavy cream
6 ounces prosciutto, cut into ¼ inch dice
salt and black pepper
2 tablespoons lard or butter or olive oil
6 tablespoons chopped fresh chives

Preheat oven to 475 degrees. Wash potatoes and bake in the oven 1 hour, or until quite done. Remove from oven. While still hot, slit each potato from end to end and scoop out centers into a large bowl. Use a kitchen glove or dish towel to protect hand. Add softened rillettes to the bowl and mix with fork until well blended but not puréed. Beat or whisk in cream. Stir in prosciutto and add salt and pepper to taste. Refill potato shells and rub skins with fat or oil. Potatoes will keep wrapped and refrigerated 3 days.

To finish, preheat oven to 450 degrees. Moisten skins with olive oil if dried out. Bake potatoes 20 to 30 minutes, until skins are crisp. Serve piping hot sprinkled with chopped chives.

CHICKEN PIE PIG-BY-THE-TAIL

This version of chicken pie is an adaptation of a dish from the Franche-Comté region of France. Sweetbreads, the surprise element in the recipe, may seem optional but are actually integral to the rest of the ingredients; the fullness of flavor is lost without them. We use fresh shiitake, or Black Forest, mushrooms to add an earthy and peppery taste. Both dried Italian porcini mushrooms, available in specialty shops, and fresh chanterelles, available by a stroke of luck, work well, as do dried shiitakes. Since there is no flour thickening in the recipes, the cream must be heavy to avoid a too thin sauce. If a good quality heavy cream with a high butter fat content is not available, start with 2 cups of a lighter heavy cream and thicken by reducing it over medium high heat to 1½ cups. Or start 2 days before and make crème fraîche by stirring 1 teaspoon buttermilk into 1½ cups cream and allowing to sit at room temperature 36 hours to thicken. Although the instructions for the chicken pie are long because there are so many elements, total preparation time is only about 40 minutes, including making the pastry. The pie is especially good cold.

——————————— Dinner for 6 or a buffet dish for 10 ———————————

For the pastry dough:

- 1 cup plus 2 tablespoons unbleached, all purpose white flour, not sifted
- ⅛ teaspoon salt
- 5 tablespoons butter, or 3 tablespoons butter plus 2 tablespoons rendered duck or pork fat, at room temperature
- 1 to 1½ tablespoons cold water

- 2 pairs veal sweetbreads, about 1½ pounds
- 3 whole chicken breasts, ¾ to 1 pound each
- 2 slices of mild ham, ¼ inch thick each
- 1 pound fresh mushrooms, or 1 ounce dried
- 2 shallots, peeled and sliced into thin rounds

5 tablespoons butter
1 teaspoon fresh thyme leaves, or ½ teaspoon dried
½ teaspoon white pepper
½ teaspoon salt
juice of ½ lemon
¼ cup brandy
1½ cups very heavy cream or crème fraîche

For glazing the crust:
1 egg yolk
1 teaspoon cream, half and half, or milk

To make the pastry, measure flour and salt into a medium size bowl. Cut butter into bits and add to flour. Using fingers or two forks, work flour and butter together rapidly until little balls form throughout the mixture. Add 1 tablespoon water and gather dough into a smooth ball. Add up to ½ tablespoon more water if dough is too dry to stick together: this depends on how soft the fat is and what the humidity and temperature are when making the pastry; colder fat and colder and drier air will require a bit more water for ingredients to cohere. Wrap in plastic wrap or wax paper and refrigerate 2 hours before using. Pastry may be made 2 or 3 days in advance and refrigerated until use; in this case, it should be wrapped in plastic wrap.

To prepare meats, place sweetbreads in a saucepan and cover with water. Bring to a boil, reduce heat, and simmer gently until sweetbreads are firm, about 40 minutes. Drain, and cool. Peel off outer membranes and filament from undersides, then slice sweetbreads ¼ inch thick. Set aside. Bone chicken breasts if butcher has not already done it and set aside. Cut ham into julienne strips and set aside.

To prepare fresh mushrooms, wipe off dirt and slice them. If using dried mushrooms, rehydrate in enough water to cover until soft, about 15 minutes, then squeeze out water and slice mushrooms. Set aside.

In a skillet, melt 4 tablespoons butter over medium high heat. Add chicken breasts, skin side down, and sprinkle with thyme, white pepper, and salt. Sauté, turning once, until chicken juices just begin to run golden but are still tinted rose, about 9 or 10 minutes. Remove chicken to a plate where juices can collect, and set aside.

Add 2 tablespoons butter to the skillet and sauté shallots until transluscent. Add mushrooms, ham, sweetbreads, and lemon juice. Stir together, then add brandy and ignite it. Stir until flames die out, then add cream. Bring to a boil and reduce rapidly for 5 minutes until the sauce is thickened and creamy. Correct salt and pepper seasoning.

To assemble, cut chicken breasts lengthwise into 1 inch wide strips and place in one layer on the bottom of a deep pie dish 10 to 12 inches in diameter. Add any accumulated juices. Pour cream mixture over chicken. Set aside to cool.

On a well floured surface, roll out pastry dough into a round large enough to overhang pie dish by 1 inch. Transfer pastry to pie dish and pinch a decorative edge all around to seal. Mix egg yolk with cream, half and half, or milk, then brush onto pastry. Pie may be chilled, then covered with plastic wrap and refrigerated overnight or it may be cooked right away. If refrigerated, remove 30 minutes before cooking.

To cook, preheat oven to 400 degrees. Bake pie 35 minutes, or until crust is golden. Serve immediately or chill overnight and serve cold. Will keep refrigerated and covered with plastic wrap up to one week.

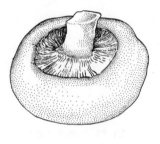

Mushroom

PEKING DUCK WITH CUMBERLAND SAUCE

Both the Oriental version, available fresh with head and neck intact in Chinese markets, and the Long Island version, available fresh or frozen in most supermarkets, of the Pekin duck breed are suitable for this recipe. Some prefer the Chinese duck for its gamier, slightly drier taste, while others prefer the Long Island for its more succulent meat. If using frozen Long Island duck, unwrap and defrost in the refrigerator overnight. Though the procedure for this recipe is long, requiring a day's time, off and on, it is not overly difficult in this version, which does not require pumping air under the skin. The hardest part is rigging a way to hang the ducks in a well ventilated spot 70 degrees or cooler. The accompanying Cumberland sauce is an excellent item to have on hand as it will keep a long time and can be used in many ways.

————————— Dinner for 6 or a buffet platter for 15 —————————

2 ducks, 4½ to 5 pounds each
water
1 cup honey
4 green onions, cut into 2 inch pieces,
    tops included
4 slices ginger root

Coriander

For the garnish:

4 green onions, shredded into long strips, tops included
6 sprigs coriander, leaves only, stems discarded
1 good eating orange, sliced as thin as possible

Half fill an 8 quart pot with water and bring to a boil. Place ducks breast side up on a counter. With hands, massage ducks and wiggle legs and thighs to loosen skin from meat; unfold wings and pull away from body to loosen skin under wings. Remove giblets if there are any and set aside. Remove excess fat from cavities and set aside to render for other uses. With a cleaver, remove heads and feet if still intact and add along with any giblets to poultry stockpot. Tie neck of each bird at neck cavity with strong kitchen string. Hold ducks by strings and immerse them in boiling water several times to scald. Hang by strings to dry for 2 hours.

After 1½ hours, half fill the pot with fresh water, add honey, 4 green onions and ginger root, and bring to a boil. When ducks have hung 2 hours, dip each several times to coat well. Rehang 4 hours. Ducks may be refrigerated, loosely covered, overnight. Remove from refrigerator 45 minutes before cooking

To cook, preheat oven to 475 degrees. Place ducks breast side up on racks in roasting pans to keep them above fat rendered during cooking. Pull wings out, away from bodies. With a knife point, prick breasts of each bird in three or four places. Escaping fat will self baste ducks as they cook. Place in the hot oven. After 20 minutes, reduce heat to 350 degrees and roast 30 minutes more.

Carefully turn ducks breast side down, taking care not to tear the skin. Roast 30 minutes more, then carefully turn breast sides up again. Raise oven heat to 475 degrees and cook 10 minutes more. Ducks are cooked after 1½ hours, or when skin color is deep reddish brown and an instant reading meat thermometer registers 200 degrees in thigh. Remove and carve immediately to serve warm, or let cool and refrigerate to serve cold. Will keep 5 days refrigerated and covered with plastic wrap.

To carve, use a boning knife to sever wings from bodies at shoulder joints. Sever legs from thighs at joints, then sever thighs from bodies at backbone joints. Carve breast and wishbone meat into thin slices. Sever breast and wishbones from backs and discard. Cut backs in half across the bone.

To serve, arrange duck pieces decoratively on a large serving platter. Dot with Cumberland sauce, then strew shredded green onions, coriander leaves, and orange slices over the top. Accompany with Cumberland sauce.

CUMBERLAND SAUCE:

rind of 1 orange
rind of 1 lemon
2 ounces blanched almonds
4 tablespoons orange juice, about 1 small orange
2 tablespoons lemon juice
⅓ cup yellow raisins
⅓ cup dried currants
8 ounces red currant jelly
2 tablespoons tawny Port

Remove rinds from orange and lemon with a zester, or use a potato peeler to remove rinds, and then chop. If you have the patience, finely shred rinds with a sharp paring knife; the effect will be nicer. Set aside.

Roughly chop almonds with a chef's knife, or swirl in a food processor 20 seconds. Place a dry sauté pan over high heat until quite warm, then toss in almonds and toast, stirring constantly, until they are browned and the aroma is released. Turn into a nonreactive saucepan and add rest of ingredients, including citrus rinds. Slowly bring to a boil, stirring frequently. Simmer over low heat about 20 minutes until a candy thermometer registers 215 degrees. Chill several hours before serving. Thin with a little citrus juice if sauce is too thick when chilled. Makes about 1¾ cups.

MARTI'S BEEF BRISKET WITH SAUERKRAUT

Beef brisket varies widely in qualities of taste and texture. Too lean or too trimmed a brisket results in dry, stringy meat. Purchase your brisket from a kosher or other good butcher if possible. Otherwise, choose from the supermarket one that has a layer of fat on the outside and weighs close to 5 pounds. Marti's brisket with sauerkraut is a good refrigerator dish; make it for a smaller group than 16 and reheat the leftovers all week. Beef brisket is also good cold; use in a composed salad or for school lunchbox sandwiches.

--------------------- Dinner for 16 ---------------------

4½ to 5 pounds fresh beef brisket, with a bit of fat on outside
2 teaspoons freshly ground black pepper

2 tablespoons butter
¼ pound sliced bacon (see page 118) or pancetta, each strip cut in 4 pieces
½ pound yellow onions, peeled and sliced ¼ inch thick

3 pounds fresh sauerkraut, homemade if possible (see page 147)
¾ cup dry white wine
1 teaspoon freshly ground black pepper
water

Rub pepper over surface of brisket and set aside. Melt butter in a heavy nonreactive pot large enough to hold brisket and sauerkraut. Sauté bacon pieces in butter, without browning, 5 minutes. Remove to a plate and reserve. Add onions to pot, stir to coat well with fat, and cook without browning until wilted. Remove pot from heat. Pierce brisket all over with a fork or metal skewer and place fat side up in pot.

Taste sauerkraut. If too salty or briny, rinse lightly with cold water, pressing out excess liquid. Spread sauerkraut over brisket. Add wine, pepper, reserved bacon, and enough water barely to cover sauerkraut. Bring liquid to a boil, cover pot, and cook over low heat 5 hours. Turn meat several times during cooking, covering with sauerkraut each time. Remove from heat. If time allows, cool and refrigerate overnight in the cooking pot to intensify flavor. Next day, reheat slowly over low heat, about 45 minutes.

To serve, slice brisket as thin as possible; use a very sharp knife to avoid shredding meat. Accompany with the sauerkraut, boiled, parslied potatoes, sour cream, and fresh horseradish sauce.

FRESH HORSERADISH SAUCE:

Grate ½ pound peeled fresh horseradish into a pottery or glass bowl. Stir in 2 tablespoons red wine vinegar and 2 tablespoons cream. Horseradish sauce will keep, refrigerated, for several days.

■ ■

GIGOT D'AGNEAU

*Leg of lamb, boldly seasoned and roasted to medium rare, makes an excellent cold meat for a medium size buffet or picnic. If the occasion calls for two sauces, serve **rouille** (see page 231) along with the mint sauce suggested here.*

———————— Dinner for 8 or a picnic or buffet dish for 16 ————————

1 leg of lamb, 8 to 9 pounds, trimmed and without pelvic bone

For the stuffing:

¼ cup chopped fresh parsley
1 teaspoon fresh thyme leaves, or ¼ teaspoon dried
1 teaspoon fresh rosemary leaves, or ⅛ teaspoon dried
1 teaspoon fresh lavender leaves, or ⅛ teaspoon dried
4 garlic cloves, peeled and minced
1 teaspoon salt
1 teaspoon black pepper
2 tablespoons olive oil

1 tablespoon olive oil to rub on outside of meat

Have butcher remove pelvic, leg, and shank bones from lamb. Or, do it yourself following the instructions in the **lamb ham** recipe (see page 120), working around shank bone to remove it also. Trim some but not all fat from the outside and remove the large chunk of fat from inside center.

Preheat oven to 475 degrees. In a small bowl mix together the ingredients for stuffing. Place lamb open side up and spread stuffing over surface. Fold shank meat flap into center then fold opening together and tie across center with string. Tie neatly and securely in several more places in whatever direction forms a neat round roast. Rub outside with olive oil.

To cook, place open side down on a baking sheet and roast 10 minutes. Reduce oven heat to 350 degrees and roast 1 hour and 5 minutes, or until an instant reading meat thermometer registers 140 degrees. Remove from oven and let rest 10 to 15 minutes so juices settle.

To serve warm, slice 1/4 inch thick, removing strings as you go. Accompany with fresh mint sauce. To serve cold, let cool completely, wrap, and refrigerate overnight, up to 5 days. Remove strings and slice 1/8 inch thick. Accompany with fresh mint sauce.

FRESH MINT SAUCE:

1 cup white vinegar
1/4 cup white sugar
1 tablespoon black peppercorns, cracked
1 shallot, peeled and minced
1 cup fresh mint leaves, cut crosswise into 1/16 inch
    strips

In a small nonreactive saucepan, heat vinegar and sugar to boiling. Add peppercorns and shallot and remove from heat. Pour over mint leaves in a small bowl and let steep 10 minutes before serving. Will keep refrigerated 1 week.

FRESH LEG OF PORK GRILLED WITH GREEK GARLIC PASTE

Pork, garlic, and rosemary are often found together in Italian cuisine. In this variation, an unboned fresh leg of pork (sometimes called fresh ham) is first marinated overnight in olive oil with garlic and rosemary, then grilled with a coating of Susanna's garlic paste, called skordalia in Greek cuisine. The result is a tender, subtly flavored meat suitable to many sauce combinations. The leg of pork may also be cooked in the oven, although with some loss of flavor. The timing will be about the same, starting with a 475 degree oven for 15 minutes, then a moderate heat of 350 degrees for the remaining time. If necessary, increase heat to brown meat for the last 15 minutes or so. Such a grand cut of meat deserves two sauces. For an exotic taste contrast, serve with both the Greek garlic paste and **Gail's loquat chutney** *(recipe follows).*

--------- Dinner for 20 or a buffet dish for 35 ---------

15 to 18 pound fresh leg of pork, skinned

2 cups olive oil
10 garlic cloves, peeled and mashed
2 teaspoons fresh rosemary leaves, or 3/4 teaspoon dried
1/2 cup salt

For the Greek Garlic Paste:

1 large russet potato
2 ounces blanched almonds
20 garlic cloves, peeled and roughly chopped
3/4 cup olive oil
2 tablespoons red wine vinegar

Remove skin and trim most of the fat from the leg of pork. Reserve skin and fat trimming to render lard and make cracklings. In a bowl, mix together olive oil, the smashed garlic, and the rosemary. Rub salt all over pork, then place it in a plastic kitchen bag. Pour the olive oil mixture over the pork in the bag and turn leg over to coat well. Close bag with tie, string, or knot, eliminating air pockets first. Place in refrigerator 24 hours, turning three times.

To make Greek garlic paste, peel and quarter potato. Place in a small pot, cover with water, and bring to a boil. Cook over medium heat until quite done, about 20 minutes from time potato goes in pot. While potato cooks, prepare other ingredients. Swirl almonds in a food processor or blender to pulverize. Set aside. Peel garlic and chop up a bit. Add to almonds. When potato is cooked, drain, let dry 10 minutes, then add to almonds and garlic. Add olive oil and red wine vinegar and process until ingredients are blended. Set aside. Sauce should be finished while potato is still warm or it will be sticky instead of fluffy. Also, this sauce is best used the same day, before the garlic breaks down and becomes ammoniated.

To cook leg of pork, prepare fire and let it burn to the white coal stage with a few specks of red, about 35 minutes. You will need about 5 pounds of mesquite to start the fire and 1 to 2 pounds more to boost fire later. Remove leg of pork from plastic bag and wipe off. Arrange coals in two piles at edges of grill bowl and place the leg of pork in the center, not directly over coals. Cover with grill lid or aluminum foil. Cook 2 hours. Spread about ½ cup Greek garlic paste over top and sides of pork. Boost the fire with fresh mesquite, cover the meat again, and cook 50 minutes to 1 hour more, until an instant reading meat thermometer registers 155 degrees in the center of the thickest part of the leg.

To carve, hold a knife perpendicular to the bone and cut into ¼ inch thick steaks. Accompany with crisp oven roasted potatoes, the remaining Greek garlic paste, and Gail's loquat chutney or another sauce to suit your whim.

GAIL'S LOQUAT CHUTNEY:

2 medium onions, peeled and cut into ¼ inch thick
   rings
4 garlic cloves, peeled and halved
2 little hot chilies, red or green, minced
2 inches fresh ginger root, peeled and cut into ¼ inch
   thick slices
3 cups, about 1½ pounds, halved and pitted loquats or
   cubed cantaloupe without rind
1 medium pineapple, peeled and cubed, including core
3 Granny Smith apples, unpeeled, cored, and cubed
juice and chopped rind of 1 lemon
¾ cup white cider vinegar
¾ to 1¼ cups sugar

Place all ingredients except sugar in a large heavy nonreactive pot.
Add ½ cup sugar. Bring to a boil then reduce heat to maintain a simmer
and cook 30 minutes. Taste for sweetness and add up to ½ cup more
sugar, depending on personal taste and the sweetness of the fruit being
used. Cook 15 to 30 minutes longer, until fruit just begins to lose its
shape. With a strainer, transfer fruit to a bowl and set aside.

Taste juices and add up to ¼ cup more sugar if desired. Reduce juices
over medium heat until thickened and beginning to caramelize on bottom
of pot. Cool completely, then mix in fruits. Store in the refrigerator up
to 2 months. Makes about 1½ quarts.

ROAST BEAST

We include our recipe for cooking a whole top round of beef for that rare occasion when you need a centerpiece roast for fifty or so people.

—————————— For a buffet dish for 50 to 60 people ——————————

whole top round of beef, 15 to 18 pounds, preferably
   prime beef
3 tablespoons salt
3 tablespoons black pepper, cracked
10 garlic cloves, peeled and slivered
½ pound fatback, cut into ¹/₁₆ inch thick slices, for
   barding

Rub top and side surfaces of meat with salt and pepper, patting in with palm. Spread garlic slivers over top. Arrange fat slices over top and tie roast at 2 inch intervals, starting in center and working out to ends. Place in a roasting pan and set aside unrefrigerated 1 hour.

To cook, preheat oven to 475 degrees. Place roast in the hot oven. After 15 minutes, reduce oven heat to 350 degrees and continue cooking 1 hour, or until instant reading meat thermometer registers 80 degrees in the center and 115 degrees 2 inches from ends. Meat will be beautifully rare all the way through. Remove from oven and let rest 20 to 30 minutes if serving warm. Or cool completely, cover, and refrigerate overnight. Roast will keep wrapped and refrigerated up to 1 week.

To serve, start at wider, which is the better, end and slice across the grain as thin as possible.

COLD
COMPOSITIONS

hat's in a salad? An olde English receipt quoted in the Oxford
English Dictionary loosely describes:

*Salat. Take persel, sawge, garlec (etc.) . . . waiche hem clene and
myng hem well with rawe oile, lay on vynegar and salt, and serve it forth.*

No mention of lettuce, but presumably the et cetera is anything that
goes well with the essential herbs, oil, and vinegar to produce a pleasing
fresh food composition. With a well stocked pantry, an assemblage of
fresh vegetables (and perhaps a leftover joint of meat or some glisteningly
fresh fish) can become a source of inspiration. Keeping in mind seasonal
harmonies of color, texture, and taste, the cook may give free rein to
imagination in composing cold salad plates.

Acid: Vinegar and lemon and lime juice provide tartness and aroma in a salad composition. A good **red wine vinegar** and fresh **lemons** are basic pantry stock for composing cold dishes. If you wish to exercise your imagination in a more expansive manner, add **balsamic vinegar** (deep, smoky, concentrated flavor), **white tarragon vinegar** (sharp, anise flavor), **rice wine vinegar** (slightly sweet and sharp flavor), and fresh **limes** (clean, citrus aroma) to your inventory.

The recipes in this chapter reflect our bias in favor of mildly tart cold dishes with an emphasis on herbs, oils, and other seasonings. Amounts for the acid component in these dishes should be varied according to the flavor of the vinegar or lemon being used, the taste of the cook, and the heat of the day.

Oil: Oil provides nutty or fruity flavor, sometimes aroma, and particularly texture. **Peanut oil** is an excellent salad oil, light both in flavor (mildly nutty) and texture (medium denseness). **Walnut oil,** imported from France and available in gourmet food boutiques, adds a heavier nutty flavor, especially good with duck or lentils. **Sesame oil,** which is quite viscous, mixes well with peanut or a light olive oil to provide a complex flavor. Use a **light olive oil,** such as Sasso brand imported Italian olive oil, for a mildly fruity rather than a nutty taste. Stock a denser French, Italian, or California **extra virgin olive oil** for when you want a more assertive fruity and aromatic olive flavor.

Herbs: Flavoring herbs and salad greens are a major tool for whimsy in salad making. The leaves and flowers of fresh herbs, whole or shredded rather than pulverized or minced, provide not only color, texture, aroma, and flavor, but also pleasant curiosity to salad compositions. Fortunately, American markets now often stock more than parsley and watercress in the fresh herb department.

The greatest joy, however, comes from plucking your own. Growing fresh herbs, in the ground or in pots, is the easiest thing to do if you have a warm sunny spot, indoors or out. For a basic variety, try a small **Greek bay tree** (fresh bay leaves are a genuine treat and very handy in Winter when other herbs are not at their best), **thyme, sage, oregano, Italian parsley, coriander, mint,** and **chives.** Add **French** or **winter tarragon, chervil,** and **basil** during the warm season. If you have more room, add **rosemary, dill, fennel, lavender, spinach,** and **lettuces** such as red leaf, romaine, Boston or butter, rocket (arugula), and lamb's lettuce (mâche). Your meals will be enhanced as never before.

Other Ingredients: In addition, we always have on hand **eggs** for whipping up a mayonnaise, **onions, shallots, garlic, salt-packed anchovies, capers,** a variety of **olives, Dijon mustard,** fresh **chilies,** and **soy sauce.**

VEGETABLES

Cook green vegetables rapidly in small batches, immersed in plenty of boiling water to retain freshness and color. We prefer this method to steaming, which has a tendency to toughen the vegetables unless they are quite small, tender, and fresh from the garden to begin with. Cooking times vary according to freshness and age. A young green bean from the garden, undefiled by refrigeration, will cook in 1 minute, whereas hothouse green beans from the market in Winter will take 5 or 6 minutes to cook to the same degree. Times given in the following recipes are for fresh market vegetables in season. If the dish is prepared a day in advance of serving, dressing is added at the last minute to avoid bleaching by vinegar or lemon.

■ ■

PEAS AND PODS

For 6 to 8 as a side dish

3 pounds English peas, shelled
1 1/2 pounds Chinese, sugar snap, or snow peas

For the dressing:

3 large shallots, peeled and minced
3 1/2 tablespoons lemon juice
1/4 teaspoon salt
6 tablespoons light olive or peanut oil

leaves of 8 sprigs of coriander
freshly ground black pepper

1/4 pound pancetta, sliced 1/8 inch thick and cut crosswise at 1/4 inch intervals

To prepare vegetables, bring a large pot of water to a boil. Snap off "caps" of pea pods, pulling off strings from inside seams with the cap. When water is rapidly boiling, drop in English peas and remove as soon as most peas are floating on the surface. Rinse under cold, running water until heat is gone. Set aside to drain in a strainer or colander. Bring water back to a rapid boil, drop in pea pods, and cook 1 minute, or until they puff out. Remove, rinse under cold water, and set aside in a strainer or colander. If preparing in advance, spread in one layer on cloth toweling, cover, and refrigerate. Dress just before serving to avoid bleaching green color with lemon juice.

To prepare dressing, mix shallot with lemon juice and salt in a bowl, then swirl in olive oil.

To serve, dry peas and pods on paper or cloth toweling, then toss together in a bowl with the coriander leaves and black pepper to taste. Set aside. Over medium high heat, fry pancetta until crisp then remove to paper toweling. Toss peas and pods with dressing and sprinkle pancetta over top.

SWEET AND SOUR LEEKS

---------- For 6 ----------

3 bunches tender young leeks
1/2 lemon
2 sprigs fresh thyme, or a pinch of dried
water

For the Sweet and Sour Sauce:

1 garlic clove, peeled and roughly chopped
1/2 medium onion, peeled and roughly chopped
1 teaspoon Dijon mustard
1 tablespoon aromatic honey
1/2 teaspoon red chili flakes
1/4 cup tarragon vinegar
1/4 cup lemon juice
1 cup peanut or light olive oil

2 teaspoons fresh thyme leaves
1 tablespoon chopped fresh parsley
1 tablespoon chopped fresh chives

Leek

To prepare leeks, trim root ends and tops, leaving about 4 inches of the green leaves. Reserve remaining leaves for stock. Halve leeks, then shred lengthwise into 1/4 inch wide strips. Immerse in plenty of cold water, swirl about, and let sit several minutes while dirt sinks to the bottom. Lift out, and repeat twice with fresh water.

In a nonreactive pot, place lemon, thyme, and enough water to reach a depth of 4 inches. Bring to a boil. Cook leeks in two or three batches, 2 or 3 minutes each. With a wire strainer, transfer each batch to a dish lined with a cloth towel and large enough to spread leeks in one layer. Cool, cover, and refrigerate several hours or up to 2 days.

To prepare sauce, blend ingredients in a blender or food processor. Or mince garlic, grate onion, then vigorously whisk together with the other ingredients. Stir thyme, parsley, and chives into sauce. Transfer leeks to a serving bowl, add sauce, toss, and serve.

181

RED BELL PEPPERS WITH GARLIC

These are two delicious preparations for red bell peppers with garlic, quintessential and satisfying peasant food. Neither version requires peeling the peppers, and both keep well up to 2 weeks.

--- For 6 ---

Sautéed:

3 pounds firm red bell peppers, halved, cored, and sliced
    into ½ inch wide strips
½ cup light olive oil
¼ cup extra virgin olive oil
2 heads garlic, cloves separated, but not peeled

2 tablespoons fresh oregano leaves, or 2 teaspoons dried
salt
freshly ground black pepper

Heat olive oils in a large skillet; add peppers, garlic cloves, and oregano. Lightly season with salt and pepper. Sauté over medium heat 35 minutes, stirring from time to time, until peppers are cooked but still hold their form. Remove to a bowl. Fish out garlic cloves, peel, and mix in with peppers. Serve hot, warm, or cold, accompanied with warm French or Italian bread on which to spread the garlic and dip into the olive oil.

Marinated:

3 pounds firm red bell peppers, quartered, seeds and
    cores removed

4 heads garlic, cloves separated, peeled, and halved
    lengthwise
5 cups white vinegar
5 cups water

¼ cup olive oil
6 bay leaves
1 tablespoon salt

Place peppers in a nonreactive container large enough to hold them in one layer. Place remaining ingredients in a nonreactive pot, bring to a boil, cover, and simmer 15 minutes. Pour over peppers, allow to cool, then refrigerate overnight. Will keep refrigerated in the brine several weeks.

SUMMER GREEN BEANS WITH NEW GARLIC AND BEST OLIVE OIL

Tender Summer green beans do not need much adornment; a little fresh garlic and your best extra virgin olive oil with some salt and pepper makes an excellent salad or side dish for almost any meal. Or for a light first course, garnish the dressed green beans with some fresh Parmesan cheese shaved with a cheese cutter, dribble a little more olive oil over the top, and accompany with warm French or Italian bread.

--- For 6 ---

1½ **pounds tender, young green beans—Blue Lakes, Kentucky Wonders, or Haricots Verts**

2 **medium new garlic cloves, peeled and minced**
salt
freshly ground black pepper
¼ **cup extra virgin olive oil**

To prepare green beans, bring a large pot of water to boil. Trim top ends, then slice beans lengthwise in half unless they are very small, in which case, they should be left whole. In three batches, cook them 2 to 4 minutes, depending on size and freshness of beans, until limp and tender but still a little crunchy. Bring water back to the boil between batches. Rinse each batch under cold water until the beans are tepid. Set aside in a strainer or colander to drain until ready to serve. Refrigerating will spoil the fresh flavor.

When ready to serve, dry beans on paper or cloth toweling. Toss with garlic and salt and pepper to taste. Add olive oil and toss again.

ARTICHOKES WITH GARLIC AND ANCHOVY DRESSING

This dish is good with any size artichoke from baby to jumbo. The cooking time varies, of course. So does the number of artichokes cooked, according to how the dish is to be used in the meal. Baby artichokes may be left whole, the entire vegetable being edible if the tough outside leaves and thorny tops are removed. If larger artichokes are used, scoop out the inedible chokes from the centers after cooking, then pour the dressing over the artichokes without tossing.

——————————— For 6 as part of an antipasto plate ———————————

For cooking the artichokes:
    1 lemon, halved
    2 heads garlic, unpeeled and halved
    2 sprigs fresh oregano, or 1 teaspoon dried
    2 teaspoons salt
    4 quarts water

    30 baby, 4 large, or 2 jumbo artichokes

    4 salt-packed anchovies, halved and cleaned, or 8 oil-
        packed anchovy fillets
    1 cup light olive oil
    salt
    freshly ground black pepper

    3 lemons

Place ingredients for cooking artichokes in a large nonreactive pot, squeezing the halved lemon as you add it. Cover the pot and bring to a boil.

To prepare baby artichokes, remove one or two layers of outside leaves, until tender light green leaves are exposed. Trim bottom ends and cut off thorny tops down to the light green, tender part of leaf. If using large artichokes, halve them and cut off thorny tops. If using jumbo artichokes, quarter them and cut off thorny tops. Drop artichokes into rapidly boiling seasoned water, cover, and cook 15 to 20 minutes, until quite soft but not falling apart. Carefully drain in a strainer or colander, to avoid breaking. Let them cool without disturbing at least 20 minutes, up to 1 hour. Reserve garlic. Artichokes may be dressed while still warm or lightly coated with olive oil and refrigerated up to 2 days before serving.

To prepare dressing, peel or squeeze garlic with fingers to release pulp from skins. Place pulp in a small bowl. Chop up anchovy fillets and add to garlic pulp. Mash garlic and anchovies with a fork, then whisk in olive oil. Or place garlic, chopped anchovies, and olive oil in a blender or food processor and purée. Season lightly with salt and pepper.

With a potato peeler or paring knife, remove and chop the rind from 3 lemons. Set aside. Halve 1 peeled lemon and squeeze juice over artichokes. Reserve the other 2 lemons for another use. Add dressing to the artichokes, then sprinkle the chopped lemon rind over them.

ROASTED AND MARINATED
EGGPLANT

Any shape or size eggplant is suitable for this dish, from the small rounded ones, which sometimes appear in specialty markets, to the large size more familiar in American markets. We like to use the small, elongated, dark skinned eggplants, found especially in Oriental markets, for their sweet taste and appealing appearance. The very small eggplants should be halved, rubbed with olive oil, and roasted, peeled, cut side down. The larger eggplants should be pricked once and roasted whole for 50 minutes, cooled, then peeled and cut into eighths. Flying fish roe is a wonderful, small-egg caviar, found in Oriental fish markets where ingredients for making sushi are sold.

──────────── For 6 as a salad or side dish ────────────

12 Japanese eggplants
light olive or peanut oil

For the marinade:

2 garlic cloves, crushed
2 teaspoons grated fresh ginger root
1/2 cup lemon juice
1/3 cup soy sauce

**3 ounces red caviar: salmon roe (see page 124) or flying
    fish roe**

Preheat oven to 475 degrees. Peel eggplants with a potato peeler, then halve them. Brush olive or peanut oil all over each eggplant, then place them cut sides down on a baking sheet. Bake in the oven 20 to 25 minutes, until soft but still maintaining their shape. Remove and cool.

Mix together ingredients for marinade. Place eggplants in a glass or pottery dish and pour marinade over. Let sit 30 minutes, or up to several hours, not refrigerated.

To serve, arrange eggplants on a platter, moisten with marinade, and dot each piece with a spoonful of caviar.

TOMATOES WITH BASIL

If you want to add anything besides a pinch of salt to the delicate voluptuousness of a fresh, warm, ripe tomato, fresh basil and a sprinkle each of red wine vinegar and olive oil are natural enhancements. Although it's hard to imagine tiring of this perfect taste combination, for diversity try minced fresh bay leaf (not dried, it does not have the same flavor), or tarragon (preferably fresh, but dried is a nice substitute when fresh herbs are not available). For fullest flavor from commercially raised tomatoes, bring them home and store them in a dark place for 3 or 4 days, then place them on a sunny window sill for another day before using. By ripening in this way, flavor may be encouraged forth even from hothouse tomatoes. A bowl of cherry tomatoes, halved and simply dressed, makes a lovely buffet or picnic dish; cutting them is no task with the following trick devised by my original partner Barbara, an efficiency genius.

——————————— A salad or side dish for 6 to 8 ———————————

3 baskets cherry tomatoes
3/4 cup loosely packed shredded, not chopped, fresh basil
    leaves
3 tablespoons red wine vinegar
3 tablespoons extra virgin olive oil
salt
freshly ground black pepper

To prepare tomatoes, first pull off stems, then rinse. Place all tomatoes on a cutting board in one layer and push into a square shape. Hold a sharp paring knife in one hand and use the other hand to keep tomatoes from rolling around as you pull knife toward you in more or less straight lines, halving tomatoes as you go. Tomatoes may be set aside several hours, but don't refrigerate them.

To dress, toss tomatoes with remaining ingredients and season with salt and pepper to taste. Serve without refrigerating.

For a wonderful Italian peasant style variation on the theme of tomatoes and basil, and for a satisfying way to use stale French or Italian bread, follow the same recipe using 2 pounds Roma or saladette tomatoes, cut into ¼ inch thick rounds. Toss in 1 teaspoon finely minced garlic, 6 ounces good mozzarella cheese, cut into julienne strips, and 1 cup of 2-day old French or Italian bread cut into ½ inch cubes. The bread should be fairly hard but not petrified—dry it out in the oven if it is too soft. Serve soon after tossing, while the bread is still crunchy.

MARINATED MUSHROOMS

This is a good way to treat ordinary commercial mushrooms,
which are a bit bland on their own.

————————— For about 2 pints —————————

2 pounds mushrooms

3 tablespoons light olive or peanut oil
3 garlic cloves, peeled and roughly chopped
1 tablespoon chopped fresh tarragon leaves, or 1 tea-
**   spoon dried**
1 teaspoon salt
½ teaspoon freshly ground black pepper
⅓ cup red wine vinegar

2 tablespoons chopped fresh parsley

To prepare mushrooms, plunge into a large basin of water, lift
out immediately, and drain in colander for a few minutes. Trim stems
and halve each mushroom if they are large; leave whole if they are small.
Pat dry on paper or cloth toweling.

To cook, heat oil in a nonreactive pot, add mushrooms, and stir to
coat all pieces. Add garlic, tarragon, salt, and pepper. Cook over high
heat 5 minutes. Add red wine vinegar and cook 5 minutes more. Remove
from heat and serve immediately, sprinkled with chopped fresh parsley,
or refrigerate in the cooking liquid up to 10 days

MOROCCAN CARROTS

Lightly pickled and spicy Moroccan carrots have a distinct bite which is a delight to some, but not for the timid palate.

—————————— For about 2½ pints ——————————

**2 pounds carrots, peeled and cut at 45 degree angle into
¼ inch thick ovals**

For the cooking marinade:

> **¾ cup lemon juice, 3 to 4 lemons**
> **1½ cups water**
> **1 tablespoon olive oil**
> **¾ teaspoon dried red chili flakes**
> **6 garlic cloves, peeled and slivered**
> **¾ teaspoon salt**

fresh coriander leaves for garnish

Place ingredients for the cooking marinade in a medium size nonreactive pot and bring to a boil. In two batches, cook carrots 2 to 4 minutes, depending on size. Transfer each batch to a bowl. Allow the cooking marinade to cool completely, pour over carrots, and refrigerate overnight.

To serve, lift carrots out of marinade and garnish with leaves of fresh coriander. Carrots will keep refrigerated in the marinade up to 1 week.

CELERY ROOT RÉMOULADE

Celery root, wilted and then tossed with rémoulade sauce, is the perfect side dish for pâtés and terrines. The rémoulade sauce is handy to have as a dip for other vegetables, such as broccoli and cauliflower, or for a quick hors d'oeuvre of **shrimp rémoulade** *(see page 232). The mustard and oil base will keep refrigerated indefinitely; add the herbs and mayonnaise just before using. Celery roots are available in Fall through Winter.*

For 5 cups

---

juice of 2 lemons
2 tablespoons salt
2 quarts water

2 celery roots, about 3 pounds altogether

1 cup rémoulade sauce (recipe follows)

In a nonreactive container mix together lemon juice, salt, and water. Peel celery roots. Using a chef's knife or a food processor attachment, cut roots into $1/16$ inch wide julienne strips. Submerge in lemon flavored salted water and set aside overnight, up to 5 days. Note: At season's end, less tender, woodier roots need a minimum of 2 days in the wilting brine.

To serve, drain celery root and dry on paper or cloth toweling. It may begin to turn brown as it dries, but will be bleached white again when mixed with the *rémoulade* sauce. Add *rémoulade* sauce to dried celery root and mix thoroughly.

RÉMOULADE SAUCE:

$1/2$ cup Dijon mustard
$1/2$ teaspoon white pepper

1 cup light olive or peanut oil
1 tablespoon boiling water

2 teaspoons fresh thyme leaves, or ½ teaspoon dried
1 teaspoon fresh chervil or tarragon leaves, or ½ teaspoon dried
¼ cup chopped fresh parsley
4 tablespoons mayonnaise (see page 219), or a little more if the mustard is quite sharp

Place mustard and white pepper in a bowl and slowly beat in the oil with a whisk or electric mixer. Stir in the boiling water. Sauce base will keep refrigerated indefinitely. Just whisk to emulsify if it begins to separate.

Before serving, whisk in herbs and mayonnaise. Makes about 1½ cups.

BROCCOLI WITH GREEN FETA AND YOGURT SAUCE

Broccoli is an appealing vegetable when properly prepared, that is, neither overcooked nor simply served raw. Its taste, texture, and color are best when it is briefly blanched in plenty of rapidly boiling water, rinsed to cool and stop the cooking, then chilled several hours to intensify flavor. The green sauce is a good all purpose vegetable dip. We prefer Bulgarian or Corsican feta over the Greek version which is much saltier.

--- For 4 pints ---

2 bunches broccoli

For the green feta and yogurt sauce:
1 bunch fresh spinach, leaves only
¼ pound Bulgarian or Corsican feta cheese
1½ cups plain yogurt
2 tablespoons chopped fresh dill

To prepare broccoli, bring a large pot of water to a boil. Trim ends of broccoli, remove heads, then peel stems. Slice stems ¼ inch thick at a 45 degree angle. Cut heads into bite size flowerets. When water is rapidly boiling, blanch broccoli, in two or three batches, depending on size of pot, 1 minute. Remove each batch to a strainer or colander, rinse under cold water until heat is gone, and set aside in another strainer or colander to drain. Chill in the strainer set over a bowl for several hours. If refrigerating overnight, remove broccoli to a container lined with clean cloth and cover.

To prepare the sauce, cut spinach leaves crosswise as thin as possible. Immerse in plenty of cold water, let dirt settle to the bottom, lift out, and repeat. Place wet spinach in a nonreactive pot over medium heat and stir until completely wilted. Remove to a colander, drain until cooled, then squeeze out all excess liquid. Mince with a chef's knife and set aside. Place feta cheese in a small bowl and mash with a fork. Whisk in yogurt, dill, and spinach.

To serve, arrange broccoli on a platter and pour half of the sauce over the top without mixing in. Serve remaining sauce separately.

JUDY'S CABBAGE

Judy's cabbage is a fresh tasting Winter alternative to green salad. Curly leafed Napa (Chinese) cabbage, halfway between Savoy cabbage and a firm leafed lettuce, is mild flavored and provides good texture contrast to the red cabbage.

--- For 3 pints ---

½ small head Napa (Chinese) cabbage, ¾ to 1 pound
½ small head red cabbage, about 1 pound
2 medium carrots
½ pound fennel bulb
½ cup chopped fresh parsley
¼ teaspoon salt
freshly ground black pepper
¼ cup strong red wine vinegar
1 tablespoon soy sauce
1½ tablespoons light olive or peanut oil

Remove outside leaves and cut cabbages into thin shreds. Peel then grate carrots. Halve fennel lengthwise, then slice crosswise as thin as possible. Toss vegetables first with herbs, salt, and pepper to taste. Add vinegar and soy sauce and toss. Add oil and toss. Let wilt in refrigerator up to 2 hours, then serve while the vegetables are still crunchy.

■ ■

PICKLED BEETS

Nutritious and delicious beets are good for bright color in Winter when red vegetables are scarce and not at their best.

---------------------------------- For 6 ----------------------------------

2 bunches beets with tops, about 2 pounds

For the cooking liquid:
> **2 cups red wine vinegar**
> **1 cup red wine**
> **3 cups water**
> **2 bay leaves**
> **2 cloves**
> **1 tablespoon salt**

> **1 large egg**

> **1 tablespoon olive oil**
> **salt**
> **freshly ground black pepper**

> **1 tablespoon red wine vinegar**
> **1 tablespoon olive oil**
> **salt**
> **freshly ground black pepper**

Remove and wash beet greens and set aside to use later. Place ingredients for cooking liquid in a nonreactive pot and bring to a boil. Add beets and cook, depending on size of beets, 50 minutes to 1 hour and 10 minutes, until a fork easily pierces to center. Lift out beets and cool enough to handle. Reserve liquid, which may be used another two or three times before it becomes too sweet to pickle.

To hard-cook the egg, place it in a small pot, cover with water, and bring to a boil. Cover, remove from heat, and let sit 7 minutes. Remove, cool under running water, peel, and set aside.

When beets are cool, peel then dice or slice them, as you like. Toss with 1 tablespoon olive oil and salt and pepper to taste, and set aside. Beets will keep refrigerated in the cooking liquid up to 1 week.

To serve, remove stems from beet greens, shred greens crosswise at ¼ inch intervals, and pat dry. Use stems to color brine for pickling eggs or onions. Toss greens with vinegar and oil, then with salt and pepper to taste. Arrange greens on a platter or plates, place beets on top, and garnish with sieved hard cooked egg.

WINTER GREEN BEANS WITH
TOMATO AND SHALLOT DRESSING

Green beans in Winter are not always worth bothering with except to pickle, but occasionally they are quite good if cut small, cooked rapidly, and assertively dressed.

--- For 3 cups ---

1 pound green beans

For the tomato and shallot dressing:
    **1 medium tomato, peeled, seeded, and cut into ¼ inch
        dice**
    2 large or 4 small shallots, finely diced
    3 tablespoons red wine vinegar
    5 tablespoons light olive oil
    salt
    pepper

To prepare green beans, bring a large pot of water to a boil. Trim top ends, then cut beans crosswise into ¾ inch pieces. In three batches, cook beans 5 to 6 minutes, rinsing each batch under cold running water until heat is gone. Bring water back to a rapid boil after each batch. Set beans aside in a colander or strainer to drain. (Use the same water to blanch the tomatoes for 10 seconds before peeling.)

To prepare dressing, mix diced tomatoes and shallot with red wine vinegar. Swirl in olive oil, then season with salt and pepper to taste. Set aside unrefrigerated.

To serve, finish drying green beans on paper or cloth toweling, arrange on a platter or plates, and pour dressing over. This salad is best served at room temperature soon after cooking.

POTATO SALAD

--------------------------------- For 6 ---------------------------------

2 pounds red potatoes

2 tablespoons Dijon mustard
1 bunch green onions, sliced into thin rounds
¼ cup chopped fresh parsley
1 tablespoon chopped fresh dill, or 1 teaspoon dried
1 teaspoon salt
1 teaspoon black pepper
1 cup mayonnaise (see page 219)

Halve potatoes if they are quite small, quarter them if medium size, or cut them into ¾ inch dice if large. Place in a large pot, fill with water to cover by 3 inches, set over high heat, and bring to a boil. Reduce heat to medium high and cook 25 to 30 minutes, or until potatoes are quite done in centers and skins are beginning to break away. Drain in a colander and set aside to cool without disturbing at least 1 hour.

To dress, toss potatoes first with Dijon mustard to coat well, then with green onions, parsley, dill, salt, and pepper. Add mayonnaise and blend in with hands, breaking up potatoes a bit as you mix. Serve without chilling, or refrigerate overnight.

PASTA SALADS

Limited only by the imaginations of multitudinous cooks, both professional and amateur, variations on the theme of pasta abound in contemporary cuisine. Here are two versions which are popular at Pig-by-the-Tail.

──────────────── A salad or side dish for 6 ────────────────

12 ounces dry pasta, preferably fusilli or shells

1 tablespoon olive oil

To prepare pasta, fill a 6 quart or larger pot two thirds full of water, cover, and bring to a boil. Add pasta, cover until water returns to a boil, and cook rapidly until just a hair past *al dente*. Perfectly *al dente* pasta sets up too firmly and tastes floury when cold. Drain, rinse briefly with cold water, and set aside in a colander or strainer for 30 minutes to 1 hour. Toss with 1 tablespoon olive oil and set aside, or cover and refrigerate until ready to use.

Pasta Primavera:

> **1 pound fresh ripe tomatoes, peeled, seeded, and chopped**
> **4 garlic cloves, a bit more than roughly chopped but not minced**
> **leaves of 1 bunch fresh basil, shredded crosswise**
> **salt**
> **freshly ground black pepper**
> **½ cup extra virgin olive oil**

> **grated Parmesan cheese**

Place ingredients except Parmesan in a nonreactive skillet and heat gently without boiling. Add to cooked pasta and toss. Accompany with grated Parmesan cheese, served separately.

Pasta with Mushrooms and Cream:

      2 garlic cloves, minced
      ½ cup grated Parmesan cheese
      ⅛ teaspoon freshly grated nutmeg

      3 tablespoons butter
      1 pound fresh shiitake, chanterelle, porcini, or oyster
          mushrooms, or a mixture, wiped clean and sliced
      salt
      freshly ground black pepper

      2 tablespoons butter
      2 ounces blanched almonds, roughly chopped

      1½ cups heavy cream

Toss cooked pasta with garlic, Parmesan cheese, and nutmeg. Set aside.

Melt 3 tablespoons butter in a skillet, add mushrooms, and sauté until wilted. If using fresh chanterelles, which are full of water, wilt in oven to render excess liquid, squeeze gently, and then sauté. Season lightly with salt and pepper and add to pasta. In the same skillet, melt 2 tablespoons butter and add almonds. Sauté until nutty aroma is released and almonds are beginning to turn golden. Add to pasta. Toss, add cream, and toss again. Adjust salt and pepper seasoning.

Serve preferably without chilling. If prepared in advance and refrigerated, mix in an additional ½ cup cream to thin the dressing, which will have set.

■■■■■■■■■■■■■■■■■■■■■■■■■■■■■■■■

WILD RICE WITH ENGLISH PEAS AND CHÈVRE CHEESE

This is a good accompanying dish for meats, fowl, and game any time the fresh peas are good, which is much of the year.

──────────── A side dish for 6 ────────────

1½ cups, about 6 ounces, uncooked wild rice
3 cups water
pinch of salt

2 pounds English peas, shelled

1 garlic clove, minced
3 ounces chèvre cheese, preferably Boucheron, crum-
    bled
salt
freshly ground black pepper
½ cup walnut or extra virgin olive oil

To prepare wild rice, place in a 2 quart pot, add water and salt, and bring to a boil over medium high, not high, heat. Cover, set pot on a metal stovetop trivet, and cook over medium low heat 50 minutes without disturbing. Remove from heat, set lid ajar, or drain in a colander if all liquid has not been absorbed, and let cool 30 minutes. Dress while still warm.

To prepare peas, bring a medium size pot of water to a boil, add peas, and cook until peas rise to the top, about 45 seconds. Remove and cool under cold running water. Set peas aside in a strainer or colander to drain. Dry on paper or cloth toweling and add to wild rice.

To dress salad, add garlic, chèvre, and salt and pepper to taste to wild rice and peas. Toss. Add oil and toss again.

LENTILS WITH FETA CHEESE

This is a slightly less expensive but equally delicious variation of the wild rice with English peas dish. Both are more flavorful if dressed and served without being refrigerated, but if you need to prepare in advance, toss the cooked lentils with a little oil to coat, and refrigerate up to 3 days until ready to use. French lentils are nuttier and more flavorful, but regular lentils will do.

—————————— A salad or side dish for 6 ——————————

1½ cups French lentils, about 10 ounces

5 green onions, tops included, cut into rounds as thin
    as possible
¼ cup chopped fresh parsley
⅓ cup lemon juice
salt
freshly ground black pepper
½ cup walnut or extra virgin olive oil

1 head crunchy green lettuce, such as romaine or esca-
    role, outside leaves removed
1 tablespoon lemon juice
2 tablespoons walnut or extra virgin olive oil

4 ounces Bulgarian or Corsican feta cheese
2 tablespoons chopped fresh chives or green onion tops

To prepare lentils, place them in a large pot with enough water to cover by 6 inches. Bring to a boil, reduce heat to moderate, and cook 17 to 20 minutes until lentils are cooked through but still *al dente*. Drain in a strainer or colander, rinse under cold water, and set aside to dry at least 30 minutes. Dress while still warm.

To dress lentils, toss with green onions, parsley, lemon juice, and salt and pepper to taste. Add oil and toss again. Set aside at room temperature.

To serve, arrange lettuce on a platter and sprinkle with lemon juice and oil. Heap lentils over top and garnish with crumbled feta cheese and chives or green onion tops.

FOUR FRUIT SALADS

Easy to prepare fruit salads are a welcome and refreshing change in hot weather. Here are four variations for mid to late Summer when the days are quite warm and the fruit is sweet and plentiful.

MELONS WITH LIME AND CORIANDER:

Halve, seed, and skin 1 cantaloupe and 1 honeydew melon, or a combination of any other melons that are ripe and sweet, then cut them into large chunks. Toss with 2 little green chilies, minced, the juice of 6 limes, and the leaves of 6 coriander sprigs. Garnish with thin slices of Swiss style air-dried cured beef, called *Bündnerfleisch*, or a *jambon cru*, such as Westphalian ham or *jambon de Bayonne*.

PEARS WITH RASPBERRY AND SHALLOT VINAIGRETTE:

Purée 1 basket of raspberries, then mix in 2 shallots, diced very small, and 1 tablespoon balsamic or white tarragon vinegar. Halve and core 6 firm but ripe pears, dress them with the raspberry and shallot vinaigrette, and garnish with slices of prosciutto.

PAPAYA WITH BLACK CAVIAR:

Halve and seed 3 ripe papayas, replace the seeds with 3 spoons of black caviar for each half, and garnish with lime wedges.

FIGS WITH FETA CHEESE:

Place 6 ounces Bulgarian or Corsican feta cheese, 4 ounces tiny Niçoise olives, 6 sprigs of thyme, and 3 bay leaves, preferably fresh, in enough extra virgin olive oil to half cover cheese. Marinate overnight or several days, turning from time to time. Serve surrounded by halves of green and black figs, with some of the olive oil dribbled over everything. Accompany with crusty French bread and very cold Retsina wine.

JAMBON PERSILLÉ

*The traditional Burgundian Easter dish of parslied ham encased
in a tarragon perfumed white wine aspic actually makes a fine
appetizer or light luncheon meal anytime. Jambonneaux out of
your own pickling bucket are the perfect ham to use, although
mild, already cooked ham is a good quick substitute. In this
case, the meat is not cooked in the aspic or it would disintegrate
and be flavorless; simmer the aspic ingredients for 30 minutes
only, then proceed with the recipe. If you can find it, use Italian
broad leaf parsley for the best flavor.*

——————————— A luncheon dish for 6 or a buffet dish for 12 ———————————

**2 jambonneaux (see page 109) uncooked, about 3
pounds, or 2 pounds cooked mild ham**

For the aspic:

**1 bay leaf
4 sprigs fresh parsley
2 green onions
1 celery top
2 garlic cloves, unpeeled and halved
2 cloves
10 black peppercorns
¾ cup tarragon vinegar
2 cups dry white wine
6 cups chicken stock**

**1 tablespoon unflavored gelatin
¼ cup dry white wine**

**1 cup packed finely chopped fresh Italian parsley
2 tablespoons finely chopped celery leaves
½ teaspoon chopped fresh tarragon leaves**

Soak *jambonneaux* in water to cover 15 minutes to remove salt. Place *jambonneaux* and ingredients for aspic in a 6 quart nonreactive pot. Pot should be small enough in diameter so that liquid covers *jambonneaux*. Bring to a boil, reduce heat to maintain the barest simmer, partially cover pot, and cook 3 hours. Do not allow liquid to boil or fat will emulsify and make a cloudy aspic. Remove *jambonneaux* and set aside to cool. Pour broth through a strainer lined with clean cloth into a bowl. Repeat several times to obtain a clear broth. Cool to room temperature, and set aside in refrigerator several hours or overnight.

When *jambonneaux* are cool enough to handle, separate meat from rind, fat, and bones. Rind with some fat is traditionally included with meat in *jambon persillé*; use it or not as you like. Discard bones and fat layer in any case. Roughly chop meat, and rind if using, cover, and set aside in refrigerator. If using already cooked mild ham, roughly chop and set aside in refrigerator.

When aspic broth is completely chilled, remove and discard layer of fat from top. Pour the chilled broth, which should be partially set, into a nonreactive pot without including any sediment from the bottom. Heat just to the boiling point.

Dissolve the gelatin in white wine, whisk into the broth, remove from heat, and pour through a strainer lined with clean cloth into a bowl. Ladle ½ cup into a 1½ to 2 quart glass bowl or terrine and refrigerate to set aspic. If aspic sets up too hard and is rubbery, thin with a little water. If it is too soft and will not hold its form, repeat the process adding a little more gelatin. Set aside remaining aspic to cool to room temperature. Don't allow it to set or you will have to reheat and re-cool it.

When aspic in bowl or terrine has set, remove *jambonneaux* or mild ham from refrigerator and toss with chopped herbs. Add to the bowl or terrine with set aspic and ladle in enough more aspic not quite to cover ham. Meat pieces should not float in liquid. Chill in refrigerator. When set, ladle in enough more aspic to cover surface by ¼ inch and chill to set again.

To serve, present in the container or unmold. Cut into wedges and place on top of lettuce. Accompany with French bread and a cruet of tarragon vinegar.

CHARCUTERIE SALAD

*Inspired by Elizabeth David's description of salade Cauchoise—
potatoes, celery, and ham garnished with fresh black truffle—
we created a more economical adaptation which substitutes oil-
cured black olives for the truffle. If you want to go for broke,
you will need 2 ounces of black truffle, very thinly sliced in
rounds. The truffle should be fresh or fresh frozen. Canned
truffles are not worth the money. Crunchy, red radicchio, a
plant of the chicory family, adds the perfect texture and color
contrast to the soft black and white of the olives and potatoes.
Substitute some other slightly bitter, crisp salad green such as
endive or watercress if the more esoteric radicchio is not available.*

——————— A luncheon for 6 or a buffet platter for 10 ———————

**2 pounds little new potatoes, red or white, halved if
quite small or quartered if medium size**

**½ pound saucisson à l'ail (see page 94), sliced ⅛ inch
thick, skin peeled**
**½ pound cooked pickled beef tongue (see page 113),
sliced ⅛ inch thick and julienned**
6 stalks celery, sliced crosswise ⅛ inch thick
3 ounces oil-cured black olives, pitted and halved
1 tablespoon fresh thyme leaves, or 1 teaspoon dried
¼ cup chopped fresh parsley
½ teaspoon salt
½ teaspoon black pepper

For the dressing:
2 tablespoons Dijon mustard
½ cup red wine vinegar
1 cup fruity olive oil

radicchio or other fresh, crunchy salad greens

Place potatoes in a pot and cover with water by 3 inches. Set pot over medium high heat and cook until quite done, 25 to 30 minutes. Reduce heat to moderate after water begins to boil. Drain in a colander and set aside to cool partially. Prepare other ingredients and set aside.

To prepare dressing, mix mustard and vinegar in a small bowl. Slowly whisk in oil.

When potatoes are cool enough to handle but still warm, place in a bowl and toss with one third of the dressing. Add sausage, tongue, celery, olives, thyme, parsley, salt, pepper, and another third of the dressing. Toss again. Place salad on radicchio leaves and distribute remaining third of dressing over the top.

BEEF TONGUE VINAIGRETTE

——————————— For a buffet dish for 8 to 10 ———————————

1 pound cooked pickled beef tongue (see page 113)

2 tablespoons Dijon mustard
2 tablespoons mayonnaise
3 tablespoons red wine vinegar
½ cup light olive or peanut oil
3 tablespoons minced shallots

½ bunch watercress, leaves only

Cut beef tongue across the grain into ⅛ inch thick slices. This is easiest to do if tongue is first cut in half crosswise then each half sliced from center out. Arrange on platter and set aside.

To prepare dressing, mix together mustard, mayonnaise, and red wine vinegar. Whisk in oil, then stir in shallots.

To serve, arrange watercress leaves over tongue and pour dressing over all. Accompany with warm French bread.

ROAST BEEF SALAD

En salade *is one of the best ways to use up leftover roast beef,
especially less rare, drier parts which benefit from being dressed.
Here are two variations, one French, one Oriental, each suitable
for luncheon or an appetizer course.*

--------------------- For 6 ---------------------

1 pound roast beef, julienned

Variation I:

> **1 medium purple or white onion, sliced into ⅛ inch
>   thick rounds**
> **6 ounces *cornichons,* quartered the long way**
> **¼ cup chopped fresh parsley**
> **1 tablespoon chopped fresh dill**
> **freshly ground black pepper**
> **salt**

> **1 teaspoon Dijon mustard**
> **3 tablespoons red wine vinegar**
> **4 tablespoons light olive oil**

In a mixing bowl, toss together roast beef, onion, *cornichons,*
parsley, dill, black pepper, and a sprinkle of salt. In a small bowl, whisk
together mustard and red wine vinegar. Whisk in olive oil, add dressing
to salad, and toss.

Variation II:

> **2 long green Anaheim chilies, halved, seeded, and sliced
>   thin crosswise**
> **¼ cup chopped fresh coriander leaves**
> **¼ cup chopped fresh parsley**

213

2 little hot chilies, red or green, minced
1/3 cup lemon juice
1/3 cup soy sauce

1/2 small head iceberg lettuce, cored and cut into thin
   shreds

2 tablespoons white sesame seeds

In a mixing bowl, toss together roast beef, Anaheim chilies, coriander, and parsley. In a small bowl mix together minced hot chilies, lemon juice, and soy sauce. Add to mixing bowl and toss. Spread lettuce on a platter and arrange salad on top. Let sit 15 to 30 minutes before serving to wilt lettuce.

Just before serving, toast sesame seeds in a dry skillet, stirring constantly over medium heat until they begin to pop. Sprinkle over top of salad.

SALAD OF ROAST VEAL

Simpler than the classic Italian dish, vitello tonnato, *this composition with cold veal makes an elegant presentation for an extravagant occasion such as a wedding buffet. A veal rump is rubbed with oil and roasted at high heat to the medium rare stage. This method both seals in juices and results in a rosy pink center, attractively exposed when the meat is sliced. For a smaller serving, the same dish can make elegant use of any leftover veal roast. Just reduce proportions for the dressing accordingly.*

——————————— For a buffet platter for 25 ———————————

3 pounds veal rump roast, not tied
2 tablespoons olive oil
4 garlic cloves, peeled and slivered
½ teaspoon black pepper
½ teaspoon salt

For the dressing, about 1½ cups:

3 tablespoons minced shallots
3 tablespoons capers, rinsed and squeezed out
8 tablespoons lemon juice
1 cup olive or peanut oil, or a mixture
1 teaspoon black pepper
½ teaspoon salt

For the garnish:

12 leaves fresh basil and 6 nasturtium flowers if the season is right, or substitute 12 sprigs fresh watercress, parsley, fennel, or tarragon

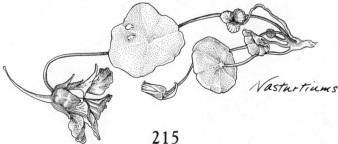

Nasturtiums

Preheat oven to 450 degrees. Rub outside of roast with olive oil, then sprinkle top with salt and pepper. Place garlic slivers down center of top. Place in a roasting pan and cook 20 to 45 minutes, depending on the thickness of the roast, until an instant reading meat thermometer registers 120 degrees. Meat will be rosy pink and not dried out when sliced. Remove, cool, cover, and refrigerate several hours or overnight. Will keep unsliced, wrapped, and refrigerated up to 5 days.

To serve, slice veal across grain as thin as possible with a knife, or have butcher machine slice it 1/16 inch thick. Arrange slices on a platter and set aside.

To make dressing, swirl shallots and capers with lemon juice in a medium size bowl. Mix in oil, then pepper and salt. Pour over veal and garnish with herb leaves and flowers as suggested, or in some other imaginative way. Accompany with warm French bread.

GIGOT EN SALADE

This is an excellent way to use leftover roast leg of lamb. Salt-packed anchovies and tiny Niçoise olives make the sauce special, but oil-packed anchovy fillets and Greek or California oil-cured black olives do nicely.

─────────────── For 6 ───────────────

For the dressing:

> 4 anchovy fillets, minced
> 1 little hot chili, red or green, minced
> 1 medium shallot, minced
> 1½ ounces black olives, pitted and roughly chopped
> 1 teaspoon chopped fresh thyme leaves, or ¼ teaspoon
>   dried
> 2 tablespoons chopped fresh parsley
> 2 tablespoons lemon juice
> 1 tablespoon fruity olive oil
> ⅓ cup light olive oil

> 24 slices cooked leg of lamb, ⅛ inch thick, about 1
>   pound

To prepare salt-packed anchovies, first rinse well. Use fingers or small knife to halve lengthwise and remove spines. Rinse again and pat dry on paper toweling. Each fish will yield 2 fillets. To store prepared fillets, immerse in olive oil, cover, and refrigerate. Will keep 2 days before they become unpleasantly strong.

To prepare dressing, mix together anchovy fillets, chili, shallot, olives, thyme, parsley, and lemon juice. Whisk in olive oils. Set aside.

To serve, arrange lamb slices on a platter and spoon dressing over.

CHICKEN SALAD PIG-BY-THE-TAIL

Our house chicken salad involves a method of roasting that results in perfect chicken every time. High heat roasting in an ordinary loaf pan just large enough to contain one bird eliminates time spent trussing, holds in juices during cooking, and turns out a chicken with golden, crisp skin and moist breast meat. In this recipe, the chicken is cooked slightly longer than you would for a bird to be served warm so that the meat is a bit drier and absorbs more flavor from the seasonings and mayonnaise. For a main dish of roast chicken, reduce the cooking time by 10 to 15 minutes, removing the bird from the oven when an instant reading meat thermometer registers 180 degrees in the thigh.

——————— For about 1 pound salad, enough for 4 ———————

For roasting the chicken:

3 to 3½ pound chicken
½ medium onion, peeled and quartered
½ lemon, quartered
3 sprigs fresh thyme, or ½ teaspoon dried
salt
freshly ground black pepper

3 stalks celery, cleaned and sliced crosswise ¼ inch
    thick
4 green onions, including tops, cut into rounds as thin
    as possible
¼ cup chopped fresh parsley
½ teaspoon salt
½ teaspoon black pepper

2 tablespoons butter
2 ounces walnut halves or pieces
1 teaspoon fresh thyme leaves, or ½ teaspoon dried

mayonnaise (recipe follows)

To roast chicken, preheat oven to 475 degrees. Pull fat out of chicken cavity and set aside to render for other use. Wipe cavity dry with paper toweling, then stuff with onion, lemon, and thyme. Sprinkle salt and pepper on outside of chicken. Place chicken in a 2 quart loaf pan or other oven dish just large enough to hold it. Place in the preheated oven and roast 1 hour and 10 minutes, or until juices from thigh run golden with no pink tinge and instant reading meat thermometer registers 195 degrees in thigh. Remove and cool enough to handle, but don't refrigerate or meat will be much harder to remove from bones.

When chicken is cool, peel off skin, then remove meat from bones, including tasty little fillets on either side of lower backbone. Break up and tear meat with hands to shred slightly. Place in a bowl and toss with celery, green onions, parsley, and salt and pepper to taste. Set aside.

In a sauté pan, heat butter until foaming, add walnuts and thyme, then sprinkle in a little salt and pepper. Stir over medium high heat until nuts are browned and aroma is released. Add to chicken and mix in. Mix in mayonnaise and adjust salt and pepper seasoning. Chicken salad will keep covered and refrigerated 2 days, but will dry out and lose its fresh taste after that.

MAYONNAISE:

2 egg yolks
1 teaspoon Dijon mustard
1 teaspoon lemon juice
1/8 teaspoon salt
1 cup light olive or peanut oil, or a mixture
2 teaspoons very hot water

To make mayonnaise, whisk or process egg yolks until thickened. Add mustard, lemon juice, and salt, and incorporate. Add oil, starting with drops and working up to tablespoon amounts. Incorporate oil thoroughly after each addition. Stir in hot water to set yolks. Set aside. Mayonnaise will keep covered and refrigerated 1 week. Makes about 1 1/4 cups.

■ ■

DALE'S CHINESE CHICKEN SALAD

Dale's version of Chinese chicken salad is a marvelously complicated dish for a festive buffet luncheon or dinner in late Spring or Summer. Dried Chinese rice noodles (mei fun), which complete the dish, are available in Oriental markets.

——————— Luncheon for 8 or a buffet platter for 12 ———————

For marinating:

4 whole chicken breasts (8 halves), boned
2 cups soy sauce
1 cup tarragon vinegar

$\frac{1}{2}$ cup peanut oil

1 head celery
4 medium cucumbers
8 young green onions
$\frac{1}{4}$ cup chopped fresh parsley
12 sprigs fresh coriander, leaves only
$\frac{1}{2}$ teaspoon salt
$\frac{1}{2}$ teaspoon black pepper
$\frac{1}{2}$ teaspoon ground coriander seed
$\frac{1}{2}$ cup tarragon vinegar
1 tablespoon sesame oil
$\frac{1}{3}$ cup olive oil

$\frac{1}{2}$ cup white sesame seeds

$\frac{1}{2}$ head iceberg lettuce

2 cups peanut oil
2 handsful dry Chinese rice noodles (mei fun)

6 sprigs fresh coriander, leaves only

Place chicken breasts and marinating ingredients in a glass or pottery bowl and refrigerate overnight.

Next day, heat peanut oil in a skillet until smoking. Remove skins from chicken breasts. Fry breasts and skins over medium high heat 25 minutes, turning once. Breasts should be dark brown and almost starting to burn; meat should be dry. Remove to paper toweling, cool, and refrigerate several hours or overnight.

Remove outer stalks from celery and set aside for soup or stock. Clean celery, then slice at a 45 degree angle into ⅛ inch thick slices. Place in a large bowl. Wash cucumbers well, then peel alternate strips to create striped effect. Cut into ⅛ inch thick slices and add to bowl. Cut green onions, including most of tops, at a 45 degree angle into ⅛ inch thick slices. Add to bowl. Add chopped parsley and coriander leaves from 12 sprigs to the bowl.

Cut breasts across the grain into ¼ inch thick slices and add to vegetables in the bowl. Crumble skins into the bowl and toss. Add salt, pepper, ground coriander seed, and tarragon vinegar and toss again. Add sesame and olive oils and toss.

Place sesame seeds in an unoiled skillet and stir over high heat until seeds begin to pop. Add to the bowl and toss.

Remove core from lettuce and shred leaves fine. Place on a large platter.

Heat peanut oil in a skillet until smoking and add half a handful of rice noodles. They will puff up and brown immediately. Turn over right away and brown other side. Remove to paper toweling. Fry remaining noodles in the same way.

Arrange chicken and vegetables on top of lettuce bed, sprinkle coriander leaves over top, then noodles over top of that. Serve immediately, accompanied with chopsticks.

DUCK SALAD NOUVELLE

Duck breast lends itself to numerous interesting hot and cold preparations. Here is one we created as a tribute to California nouvelle cuisine. The duck breast should be cooked the morning or day before serving and thoroughly chilled to allow the meat to become firm and the fat and juices to set. The rest of the duck may be roasted for a separate dish or salted down and used for **confit** *or* **duck rillettes.** *Walnut oil makes the dish special, but you may substitute peanut or light olive oil mixed with ¹/₂ teaspoon sesame oil. If Chinese peas are not available, use sugar snap peas, baby green beans, or blanched broccoli flowerets.*

———————— Hors d'oeuvre for 6 or a buffet platter for 8 ————————

breasts from 2 ducks, 4 halves
1 tablespoon walnut oil

¹/₂ pound Chinese peas

3 medium small turnips, about ³/₄ pound

8 sprigs fresh coriander, leaves only
¹/₄ teaspoon salt
¹/₂ teaspoon black pepper
2 tablespoons red wine vinegar
4 tablespoons walnut oil

2 tablespoons white sesame seeds
6 sprigs fresh coriander

Preheat oven to 475 degrees. Rub duck breasts with 1 tablespoon walnut oil and place skin side up on a rack in a roasting pan. Place in oven. After 15 minutes, reduce heat to 350 degrees and cook 10 minutes more, until an instant reading meat thermometer registers

180 degrees. Meat should be medium rare. Remove, cool, cover, and refrigerate at least 6 hours or overnight.

To cook Chinese peas, half fill a 2 quart pot with water and bring to a boil. Snap cap end off peas, removing string from inside seam along with cap. Blanch in boiling water 1 minute, until just starting to puff out. Immediately drain and rinse under cold water until cooled. Leave to drain, or wrap in a towel and refrigerate overnight.

To prepare turnips, peel with a peeler or paring knife. Shred in a food processor or use the largest hole of a hand grater. Set aside or refrigerate covered overnight.

To assemble, remove and discard bones from duck breasts and cut meat crosswise into thin slices. In a bowl, toss together duck, Chinese peas, coriander leaves from 8 sprigs, salt, and pepper. Add vinegar and toss. Add walnut oil and toss. Place two thirds of the shredded turnips on a platter or individual serving plates. Distribute duck salad evenly over turnip bed and top with remaining third of turnips. Set aside.

Toast sesame seeds in unoiled sauté pan, shaking or stirring frequently over high heat until seeds begin to pop. Sprinkle over duck salad and garnish with remaining sprigs of fresh coriander.

MUSSEL SALAD

For 3 pints
---

5 pounds fresh live mussels
2 cups water
½ cup white wine
1 bay leaf

5 celery stalks, cleaned and diced
2 tablespoons finely chopped fresh parsley
1 tablespoon fresh thyme or coriander leaves

For the dressing:

2 shallots, minced
5 tablespoons lemon juice, about 1½ lemons
freshly ground black pepper
6 tablespoons light olive oil
2 tablespoons heavy cream
salt

Place mussels in a colander and rinse well under cold running water. Put water, white wine, and bay leaf in a large pot; a 10 quart pot will hold 5 pounds of mussels, or in a smaller pot, steam in several batches. Pot should be nonreactive if you intend to use the liquid in which mussels are steamed for another purpose. Bring liquid to a boil and add mussels. Cover and steam over moderately high heat 8 minutes, shaking pot once or twice. Remove mussels with a strainer and let them cool enough to handle. Shuck mussels, removing "beards" with fingers or paring knife. Discard any mussels that have not opened.

In a medium size bowl toss together shucked mussels, celery, parsley, and thyme or coriander. At this point, dish may be covered with plastic wrap and stored in refrigerator up to 2 days. Continue when ready to use.

In a small bowl, mix together shallots, lemon juice, pepper to taste and oil. Add to mussels and toss. Add cream and toss. Add salt to taste.

To serve, arrange on a bed of lettuce on a platter or individual plates. Accompany with warm French bread.

SQUID WITH PEPPERS

The method of cleaning squid described below produces spirals instead of the more usual rounds and has the added advantage of making a laborious chore easier when preparing large amounts. The dish is best with very fresh, medium size squid.

―――――――――――――― For 6 ――――――――――――――

5 pounds squid

1 green bell pepper, halved, seeded, cored, and julienned
2 red bell peppers, halved, seeded, cored, and julienned
**2 long green Anaheim chilies, halved, seeded, cored,
    and thinly sliced into half rounds**
3 little hot chilies, red or green, minced
2 teaspoons minced garlic
**2 tablespoons chopped fresh oregano leaves, or 2 tea-
    spoons dried**
¹/₄ cup chopped fresh parsley
¹/₂ cup lemon juice
¹/₂ cup fruity olive oil
salt
freshly ground black pepper

To prepare squid, first use a small knife to remove tentacles just above eyeballs. As you go, push out hard ball from center of each tentacle. Place tentacles in a bowl and set aside. To prepare bodies, slit open lengthwise and scrape away insides with a small knife. The neatest way to do this is to set a small cutting board over newspaper so squid guts, which are quite sticky and adhesive, do not have to be cleaned off counter. When bodies are cleaned, slice each crosswise into three parts. Set aside with tentacles.

To cook squid, bring a large pot of water to boil. Have handy a large strainer or colander set over a large bowl. When water is rapidly boiling, add one third of squid and cook 90 seconds. With a wire strainer, remove squid to a colander and rinse immediately under cold running water until they are thoroughly cooled. Set aside in another colander or strainer. Allow water in pot to return to a boil and repeat process until all squid are cooked. Drain in a second colander several hours or overnight, refrigerated.

To assemble salad, toss squid with peppers, garlic, oregano, and parsley. Add lemon juice and toss, then add olive oil and toss. Season to taste with salt and pepper.

Serve with French bread and a side dish of oil-cured black olives tossed with crushed garlic, minced bay leaf, and a little olive oil.

■ ■

SALMON SALAD

This composition was inspired by the landscape of the northern California coast where salmon is fished within view of shores covered with stands of wild fennel. Here, we prepare the bulb of the domestic fennel plant à l'Italienne, garnish the dish with shimmering ruby squares of tomato gelatin, and emphasize the Italian flavor with a light aïoli sauce. This is a dish for late Fall, when salmon and fennel are both in season.

────────────── Lunch for 10 or a buffet platter for 15 ──────────────

For the gelatin garnish:

    1 cup tomato juice
    ¼ cup tarragon vinegar
    1 teaspoon Tabasco
    1½ cups water
    2 teaspoons unflavored gelatin
    ¼ cup warm water

    6 pound salmon
    3 tablespoons olive oil
    3 tablespoons lemon juice
    salt
    freshly ground black pepper
    ½ small onion, peeled and sliced into rounds
    1 lemon, sliced into rounds

For the aïoli, about 2 cups:

    2 slices of baguette or 1 slice of regular French bread
    6 garlic cloves, peeled and roughly chopped
    3 egg yolks
    ½ teaspoon salt
    1½ cups light olive oil
    1 tablespoon lemon juice

1 large head fennel, including some of the top
¼ cup lemon juice
1 teaspoon salt

Fennel with fronds

Place tomato juice, tarragon vinegar, Tabasco, and 1½ cups water in a small nonreactive saucepan over medium heat and bring to a boil. Dissolve gelatin in ¼ cup water, stir into tomato juice mixture, and remove from heat immediately. Pour through a strainer lined with clean cloth into a rectangular container. Refrigerate several hours or overnight to set. Gelatin may be prepared several days in advance and stored, covered, in refrigerator.

Butterfly salmon by inserting knife into flesh at the head end right next to the backbone. Holding knife blade next to backbone, cut down length of fish to tail. Bones and backbone are easy to remove after fish is cooked, so just leave them for now. Place salmon opened out and skin side down on a baking sheet. Rub olive oil over surface, sprinkle with lemon juice, salt, and pepper, then strew onion rings and lemon slices over top. Set aside to marinate 20 to 30 minutes.

Preheat oven to 350 degrees.

To make *aïoli*, soften bread in water to cover 10 minutes. Squeeze bread dry and place in a mortar, blender, or food processor bowl. Add garlic and pound or purée together. Add egg yolks and salt and pound or purée to form a paste. Slowly add olive oil, starting with drops and working up to tablespoon amounts. Stir in lemon juice. Set aside or refrigerate until ready to use.

To cook salmon, place in the preheated oven and bake 15 minutes or until an instant reading meat thermometer registers 115 degrees in thickest part. Remove from oven and cool 2 hours or refrigerate, covered, overnight. Salmon may be prepared up to 2 days in advance.

When ready to assemble salad, prepare fennel. Pare away dry or brown spots, remove and reserve feathery fronds, then cut bulbs into quarters. Slice crosswise as thin as possible. In a small bowl, toss fennel with lemon juice and salt. Set aside to marinate at least 30 minutes, up to 3 hours. Chop fronds and set aside.

To serve, remove bones and backbone from salmon with fingers. Lift meat off skin and arrange, in large chunks, in center of platter. Unmold tomato gelatin and cut into ½ inch cubes. Place alternating piles of fennel and tomato gelatin cubes on either side of salmon. Place dollops of *aïoli* on top of salmon, then sprinkle chopped fennel fronds over *aïoli*. Accompany with warm French bread and the remaining sauce.

TUNA WITH ROUILLE SAUCE

Fresh tuna, the beef of fish, rivals salmon in appeal even to nonlovers of fish, and it is a shame that the pervasiveness of canned tuna has all but obliterated its use in coastal regions where it is available. Rich and spicy Provençal rouille sauce is a particularly good dressing for the robust full flavor of fresh tuna. Choose a firm red bell pepper with unwrinkled skin for easier peeling. The green bell pepper garnish provides a pleasing crunchy element to the texture of the dish.

——————————— Lunch or dinner for 6 ———————————

6 fresh tuna steaks, ¹/₂ inch thick each, about 2 pounds
    altogether
juice of 1 lemon
¹/₄ cup olive oil
2 garlic cloves, peeled and slivered

6 large handsful salad greens
1 teaspoon lemon juice
1 tablespoon olive oil
freshly ground black pepper

For the garnish:

1 medium size green bell pepper, cored, seeded, and
    finely diced
12 medium size leaves fresh basil, finely shredded cross-
    wise

Place tuna steaks in a nonreactive container just large enough to hold them in one layer. Pour lemon juice and olive oil over tuna and spread garlic over top. Turn steaks over to coat with marinade and let sit 30 minutes, turning once.

If grilling, prepare fire and let it burn to the white coal stage with a few splotches of red. If baking, preheat oven to 375 degrees.

To cook tuna steaks, place them on a grill over coals or on a baking sheet, large enough to arrange steaks without touching each other, in the oven. Cook 6 minutes, or until an instant reading meat thermometer registers 105 degrees. Tuna will be medium rare. Remove from heat and assemble salad while tuna is still warm, or cool, cover, and refrigerate overnight.

To serve, toss salad greens with lemon juice and olive oil, then with freshly ground black pepper. Mix together minced green bell pepper and shredded basil. Place greens on plates or a platter. Arrange tuna steaks in the center and garnish each steak with 1 dollop each of *rouille* sauce and green bell pepper and basil mixture. Accompany with more *rouille* sauce served separately.

ROUILLE SAUCE:

2 medium red bell peppers
6 garlic cloves, peeled and crushed
4 thick slices of dry baguette or 2 slices of regular
    French bread, about 1½ ounces, broken up
1 teaspoon cayenne
¾ cup light olive oil
salt

To prepare red bell peppers, roast on a grill over hot fire or in a preheated 500 degree oven, or place over a gas flame, until skins are charred, 15 to 20 minutes depending on size and firmness. Place peppers in a paper bag, twist bag shut, and let steam 15 minutes. Peel off skins and remove seeds and cores. Roughly chop peppers.

To make the sauce, soak bread slices in water to soften, then squeeze dry. If using a food processor, place red bell peppers, garlic, bread, and cayenne in the processor bowl and purée. Slowly add olive oil, starting with drops and working up to tablespoon amounts. If using a mortar and pestle, place all ingredients except olive oil in the mortar and pound to form a smooth paste. Slowly incorporate olive oil with a whisk. Season with salt to taste. Makes a bit more than 1 cup.

SHRIMP RÉMOULADE

Grated raw zucchini and a French style rémoulade sauce seasoned with thyme replace the more typical bed of lettuce and tarragon flavored mustard sauce in this familiar New Orleans dish. A fresh chervil garnish adds a pleasantly pungent taste, if you can get it. Dijon mustards vary enormously in hotness; so do shrimps vary in taste, depending on freshness and kind. Add more mayonnaise if the rémoulade sauce is too strong for the shrimp being used. Fresh shrimp is best, of course, but fresh frozen will do for this recipe.

————————— First course for 6 or a buffet platter for 10 —————————

For the poaching liquid:

 1½ quarts water
 ½ cup red wine vinegar
 ½ cup red wine
 ½ onion, sliced
 ½ hot chili, or ¼ teaspoon dried chili flakes
 1 bay leaf
 3 sprigs fresh thyme, or ½ teaspoon dried

 3 pounds shrimps without heads, or 3½ pounds with
   heads
 1 pound zucchinis
 1 cup rémoulade sauce (see page 193)

 juice of 1 lemon
 1 tablespoon fresh chervil leaves, or 2 tablespoons
   chopped fresh parsley

Place ingredients for poaching liquid in a nonreactive pot, bring to a boil, and let simmer 1 minute. If using fresh shrimps, rinse under cold, running water and add to pot. Simmer 3 minutes, then remove to a large bowl. If using frozen shrimps, drop them while still frozen into the boiling poaching liquid and simmer 5 minutes. Drain in a colander and rinse lightly under cold water. Peel shrimps, leaving tails intact. With a paring knife, cut along the back and remove sand vein, which is actually the intestinal tract. Pat shrimps dry with paper toweling and set aside, or cover and refrigerate overnight.

Trim ends off zucchinis, then grate in a food processor or through the largest holes of a hand grater. Set aside, or cover and refrigerate overnight.

To assemble, mix grated zucchini with ¼ cup of the rémoulade sauce. Place on a platter or individual plates. Toss shrimps with lemon juice, then mix in remaining rémoulade sauce. Arrange shrimps on the zucchini bed. Sprinkle chervil leaves or chopped parsley over the top and serve chilled.

CUCUMBERS WITH SHRIMP YOGURT

For about 3 pints

For the shrimp yogurt sauce:

>1 quart plain yogurt
>1/2 pound bay or gulf shrimp, weighed after shelling and
>	deveining
>juice of 1/2 lemon
>1 tablespoon grated red onion
>1 teaspoon chopped fresh tarragon, or 1/2 teaspoon dried
>1 tablespoon red wine vinegar
>
>3 cucumbers
>salt

For the garnish:

>1/2 pound bay or gulf shrimp, weighed after shelling and
>	deveining
>juice of 1/2 lemon
>1/4 teaspoon cayenne
>
>1 tablespoon chopped fresh chives or green onion tops

To make the shrimp yogurt sauce, place yogurt in a strainer lined with clean cloth, set over a bowl, and let sit several hours or overnight to drain off whey. Place 1/2 pound shrimps in a medium size bowl, toss with lemon juice, rinse lightly, and pat dry. Mash shrimps with a fork, then stir into the drained yogurt. Stir in onion, tarragon, and red wine vinegar. Set aside.

Wash cucumbers and peel in stripes. Slice thin, toss with salt to taste, then fold into shrimp yogurt. Toss second 1/2 pound shrimps with lemon juice and cayenne, then mound on top of cucumbers and yogurt. Sprinkle chives or green onion tops over top. Serve very cold with pita or Armenian cracker bread.

ALICE'S FISH TARTAR

This delicate fish tartar is exemplary of Alice Waters' imaginative way of combining ingredients with a light but incisive touch. The fish must be pristinely fresh and should be served rather soon after preparing. Your knife should be quite sharp to avoid mashing the fish as you dice. If fresh chervil is not available, substitute half the amount of fresh coriander leaves, which provide a similar but less subtle taste.

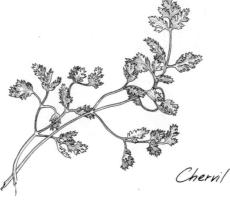

Chervil

--- For 6 ---

⅓ **pound salmon fillet, skinned**
⅓ **pound halibut or sea bass fillet, skinned**

For the dressing:

1 large shallot
1½ teaspoons lemon juice, or more if needed
2 teaspoons chopped fresh chervil leaves
1½ teaspoons chopped fresh parsley
⅓ cup mayonnaise, made with light olive oil (see page 219)
salt
pepper

6 leaves red leaf lettuce

Slice well chilled salmon and halibut or sea bass fillets ⅛ inch thick in any direction, stacking slices in several piles as you go. Next, slice into ⅛ inch thick strips, then cut across strips at ⅛ inch intervals to wind up with fine dice. Work rapidly so fish does not become too warm and mushy. Chill while preparing dressing.

To prepare dressing, score shallot at very small intervals almost but not all the way through bulb in one direction and then at right angles in another direction. Slice as thin as possible across the scored surface. Stir shallot, lemon juice, chervil, and parsley into mayonnaise.

Gently mix dressing and diced fish. Season with salt and pepper and add a few more drops of lemon juice if desired.

Serve on red leaf lettuce and accompany with croutons made from thin slices of *pain de mie* or baguette brushed on each side with olive oil and oven toasted until golden brown.

SAVORIES

*. . . including all manner of
flavorful tidbits, not sweet, but spicy,
and stimulating to the taste*

BRANDADE OF SALT COD

Brandade de morue, *salt cod paste, is a specialty of southern France, in particular Provence and Languedoc, where it appears as a slightly saltier, smoother spread with a bit less garlic. Our recipe calls for soaking the fish 48 hours, but this varies according to how salty the cod is to begin with. Taste a piece after 36 hours: it should be removed from the water when the salt is just right to the palate; longer soaking will take out too much flavor, and undersoaking will result in a dish too salty to eat. When shopping, choose very white, soft salt cod. Yellow color and hard texture mean the fish is either too old or has been cured with a harsh salt. The optional truffle makes the dish sublime, but it is already superb without.*

--- For 4 cups *brandade* ---

1 pound salt cod
1 small russet potato, about ⅓ pound
3 to 4 garlic cloves, peeled and slivered
½ cup heavy cream
½ cup olive oil
2 tablespoons lemon juice

1 ounce black truffle (optional)

To prepare salt cod, rinse thoroughly, then place in a non-reactive container and add water to cover. Soak in the refrigerator 48 hours, changing the water two or three times.

To make *brandade,* half fill a large pot with water and bring to a boil. Peel and quarter potato and add to pot. After 15 minutes, add salt cod to pot and cook 10 minutes more. Drain in a colander and let cool just enough to handle. Remove bones, then flake fish. In a food processor, or with an electric mixer, swirl together all ingredients except truffle until smooth but not puréed. Stir in the truffle if you are using it.

To serve, mound warm *brandade* in the center of a platter and surround with ¼ inch thick slices of French bread fried on both sides in olive oil. *Brandade* may be reheated in a double boiler: stir with a wooden spoon until mixture fluffs up. May be kept 2 or 3 days, but not longer without sacrificing the sweetness of the dish.

■ ■

STUFFED VINE LEAVES: TWO WAYS

Grape leaves always remind me of childhood family gatherings when my Armenian grandmother and aunts would cook mounds of delicious food for numerous people. Stuffed grape leaves, called sarma, *were always included for the best occasions: home brined Thompson seedless grape leaves, picked before the fruit had set on the vine, stuffed with lamb and rice. Children saw them as little cigars they could pretend to smoke, especially convincing with a dot of yogurt on the tip to simulate an ash. Today, in addition to the traditional Eastern Mediterranean lamb and rice stuffing, we make a wild rice stuffing to suit the tastes of our vegetarian clientele. For a gala picnic, buffet, or cocktail party presentation, serve both versions.*

──────────── For approximately 80 grape leaves ────────────

NOUVELLE VEGETARIAN STUFFING:

1½ cups, about 6 ounces, uncooked wild rice
1 cup, about 6 ounces, uncooked long grain white rice
water

2 tablespoons butter
2 ounces blanched almonds, chopped fine, not pulverized
2 ounces sun dried apricots, finely diced
3 ounces dried currants
3 ounces golden raisins

1 medium or 2 small yellow or white onions, finely
    diced
½ cup chopped fresh parsley
⅓ cup chopped fresh mint
peeled and chopped rinds of 4 lemons
¾ cup lemon juice
¾ cup olive oil

Grape leaf

To cook wild rice, place in a small pot with 3 cups water. Water should cover by ½ to ¾ inch for rice to cook properly, so choose pot size accordingly. Bring to a boil over medium, not high, heat. Cover, reduce heat to low, and cook 50 minutes without raising the lid. Follow the same procedure for white rice, using 2 cups water and cooking 17 minutes. Note: Rice cooks best if a metal stovetop trivet is used under the pot to maintain an even low heat. When rice is done, remove from heat, set cover ajar, and let sit 30 minutes to cool and steam dry.

In a sauté pan, melt butter until foaming, then add almonds. Stir until almonds begin to brown, then add apricots, currants, and raisins. Stir until raisins and currants plump up, 2 or 3 minutes. Set aside.

In a large bowl, mix together wild and white rices, separating grains with fingers. Add ingredients in sauté pan and remaining ingredients. Mix thoroughly with hands.

——————————— For approximately 50 grape leaves ———————————

EASTERN MEDITERRANEAN LAMB AND RICE STUFFING:

**1 pound lamb, shoulder meat or leg trim, or ground
lamb purchased from butcher**

½ cup uncooked long grain white rice, cooked with 1
    cup water as described in preceding recipe
1 medium onion, peeled and chopped fine
½ cup chopped fresh parsley
2 teaspoons chopped fresh oregano leaves, or ½ tea-
    spoon dried
1½ teaspoons salt
1 teaspoon black pepper
¼ cup lemon juice
6 tablespoons tomato paste

Trim lamb of large nerves and most but not all fat. Using the small grinder plate, grind lamb into a large bowl; or place purchased ground lamb in a large bowl. Add cooked rice, onion, parsley, oregano, salt, and pepper and mix thoroughly with hands. Add lemon juice and tomato paste and mix again.

To stuff grape leaves, place leaves smooth side down, stems toward you, on a counter and trim off stems with a sharp paring knife or scissors. Depending on size of leaf, place 1 to 1½ tablespoons stuffing in the center. Fold one side then the other side of leaf bottom over stuffing. Roll up a half turn, then fold sides in toward the center. Continue rolling up to make a neat cylinder. Place rolled grape leaves in deep (at least 4 inches) 4 quart roasting pan or heavy pot, or use smaller containers as long as they are deep enough to hold enough water to cover grape leaves. Push together to pack tightly as you go. Cover with one or two plates that fit inside the container to keep leaves from floating up.

To cook, fill container with water to cover grape leaves, set it over medium heat, and bring to a boil. Cook 10 minutes, remove from heat, and cool 20 minutes. Pour off water, pressing down on grape leaves to drain thoroughly. Chill in refrigerator overnight to intensify flavor. Will keep wrapped and refrigerated up to 10 days.

To serve, arrange stuffed grape leaves on a platter and dribble lemon juice and olive oil over all. Or omit the lemon, dribble olive oil over the top, and accompany with **yogurt and mint sauce** (see page 62), to which a little minced garlic has been added. Stuffed grape leaves may be served at room temperature, but they should be allowed to cool and set up a bit to intensify flavor. Reheating toughens the leaves.

STUFFED JUMBO MUSHROOMS

Stuffed jumbo mushroom caps make an excellent cocktail savory or light first course before a formal dinner. During a brief period when very good fresh snails were commercially available, we devised a New Orleans inspired version of take-out escargots, stuffed in jumbo mushroom caps and sauced with a sorrel, shallot, and anise liqueur butter. It is easy enough to prepare live snails yourself according to the instructions which follow. Collect common brown garden snails (Helix aspersa) or other edible garden snails of your region from gardens with no snail poison. Or buy live land snails in (especially Oriental) fish stores. Imported large French snails may be substituted if you do not feel like raising your own.

If snails are not to your taste, and they do seem to be out of fashion now, try the spinach and ricotta stuffing or some other variation of your own invention, for example using the last bit of sausage meat that has not been pushed all the way through the stuffer. Jumbo mushrooms have the most flavor of the regular commercial (champignon de Paris) mushrooms. Use the largest available if jumbos are not in your market.

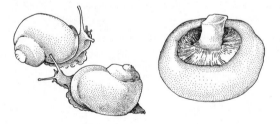

―――――――――――――――― For 12 stuffed jumbo mushrooms ――――――――――――――――

SNAILS WITH ANISE LIQUEUR AND SORREL STUFFING:

24 large or 36 small snails
1 tablespoon anise liqueur, Pernod or Herbesaint
1 teaspoon fresh thyme leaves, or ½ teaspoon dried
freshly ground black pepper

For the butter sauce:

> ½ pound butter, softened to room temperature
> 2 shallots, peeled and minced
> ¼ cup chopped fresh parsley
> ½ teaspoon anise liqueur, Pernod, or Herbesaint
> ½ teaspoon salt
> freshly ground black pepper
> few drops of lemon juice

> 1 bunch fresh sorrel, cut crosswise into ⅛ inch wide
>   strips, washed, spun or patted dry, leaves cut cross-
>   wise into thin shreds, then chopped a bit
> 12 jumbo mushroom caps
> 4 tablespoons butter, softened to room temperature
> salt

> ⅓ cup homemade bread crumbs

To prepare live snails, put them in a box with a layer of damp cornmeal on the bottom. Set a board for weight on top to keep snails from escaping. Place the box in a shady spot; if weather is hot, spray lightly with water to dampen once a day. Leave snails 72 hours to purge of any off flavors or toxic materials from previously eaten food. Rinse snails and pack again in the box, this time with plenty of fresh herbs and edible leaves such as grape, nasturtium, or lettuce. Leave in a shady spot 48 to 72 hours for them to fatten and develop flavor. Spray leaves with water once a day. When ready to cook snails, select only the active ones which have crawled up sides of the box and discard the inactive ones on the bottom.

To cook live snails, wash well under cold water. Blanch 10 minutes in boiling water seasoned with a few bay leaves, a sprig of thyme, and several garlic cloves. Drain, then pull snails out of shells. Cut or pull off and discard gall, which is the small curled sac about ¼ inch long at tail end, where snail was attached to shell. Rinse snails and pat dry. May be prepared in advance, wrapped in plastic, and stored in freezer until ready to use.

To prepare canned snails, rinse briefly under cold water and pat dry.

In a small bowl, toss prepared snails with 1 tablespoon anise liqueur, the thyme, and black pepper to taste. Set aside at least 2 hours, or refrigerate overnight.

To make sauce, cream the butter in a food processor or with an electric mixer. Add remaining sauce ingredients and blend thoroughly. Set aside until ready to use. Will keep wrapped and refrigerated up to 2 days. Soften to room temperature before using.

To prepare mushroom caps, snap out stems and reserve for another dish. Wipe caps with cloth or paper toweling, then rub outsides with softened butter. Sprinkle insides with salt and place 1 teaspoon butter sauce in bottom of each. Distribute sorrel evenly among mushroom caps, then place 2 or 3 snails, depending on size, on top of sorrel. Cover each mushroom cap with 1 tablespoon more butter sauce, then sprinkle bread crumbs over butter. May be prepared ahead to this point, wrapped, and refrigerated overnight.

To cook, preheat oven to 400 degrees. Place stuffed mushroom caps on a baking sheet in the oven and bake about 15 minutes, until butter is bubbling and mushrooms give easily when squeezed between thumb and forefinger. Serve immediately, piping hot.

SPINACH AND RICOTTA STUFFING:

**2 bunches fresh spinach, stems discarded, leaves cut
crosswise into 1/4 inch strips, washed twice in plenty
of cold water, and drained in a colander**

1/2 pound ricotta cheese
1/4 cup finely grated Parmesan cheese
2 tablespoons cream
1/4 teaspoon minced garlic
1/8 teaspoon freshly grated nutmeg
1/4 teaspoon cayenne
1/4 teaspoon salt

paprika

Place the prepared, still wet, spinach in a nonreactive pot and stir over medium heat until wilted. Drain in a colander and let cool enough to handle. With hands, squeeze out excess liquid, then mince spinach. In a food processor or with an electric mixer, blend together all ingredients except paprika.

Prepare mushroom caps as described, then fill each with 2 tablespoons spinach and ricotta stuffing. Sprinkle a pinch of paprika over top of each and bake as described above.

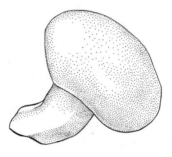

DEEP FRIED VEGETABLES TAPENADE

Tapenade *is probably the source idea for those little tins of bland chopped olives out of which the soul has been extracted and discarded. The original classic Provençal dish is an earthy, complex spread of black olives, garlic, anchovies, and capers bound with olive oil. With French bread, perhaps a little cheese, and a glass of wine, not much more is needed for a picnic except a good spot in which to enjoy the spread.* Tapenade *is also a delicious condiment sauce for grilled fish such as tuna or mackerel and a fine dip for a Mediterranean array of deep fried vegetables as we suggest here. Niçoise olives will make a milder* tapenade; *oil-cured black olives will produce a delicious dish at less expense. Sweet basil lends aromatic depth to the spread, but should be omitted when not in season—dried basil confuses the flavor without adding aroma.*

--- Cocktail savories for 12 ---

2 medium yellow or white onions, peeled and cut into
    ¼ inch thick rings
12 baby zucchinis with flowers attached, split length-
    wise to within ½ inch of tops
24 baby artichokes, outside leaves removed, tips and
    bottoms trimmed
6 tiny eggplants, quartered, or 3 Japanese or Chinese
    eggplants, cut into ½ inch thick rounds

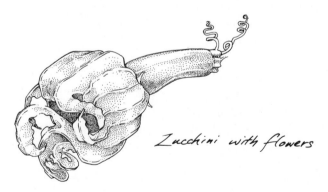

Zucchini with flowers

For the batter:

>12 eggs
>1 cup milk
>1 cup water
>salt
>black pepper

>6 cups unbleached all purpose white flour, or a little
>>more

>8 cups peanut oil

In large bowl, mix together ingredients for batter. In another large bowl, place the flour. In a deep skillet or pot, heat oil until beginning to smoke. If you feel like splurging on the oil, which cannot be reused, use two pots and twice as much oil to go faster and keep vegetables crisper. In several batches so that pieces do not stick together while frying, dip vegetables in batter, coat with flour, and drop into hot oil. Remove vegetables to paper toweling when they are done.

Serve immediately accompanied with a bowl of *tapenade*.

TAPENADE:

>1½ pounds black olives, Niçoise or oil-cured
>6 medium garlic cloves, peeled and roughly chopped
>6 anchovy fillets, preferably salt-packed
>¼ cup capers, rinsed and squeezed dry
>⅔ cup light olive oil
>1 to 3 tablespoons lemon juice, depending on your taste
>½ cup roughly chopped fresh basil leaves

Pit olives. If using Niçoise olives, first bruise each with a wooden mallet or hammer, striking hard enough to flatten olive slightly but not hard enough to crack through pit.

Swirl together all ingredients in a blender or food processor until blended but not puréed. *Tapenade* will keep refrigerated several weeks. Makes about 3 cups.

CHICKEN TIDBITS

CHICKEN WINGS ORIENTALE:

For the marinade:

>1 cup soy sauce
>1 cup white wine
>1 teaspoon dried red chili flakes
>1 tablespoon chopped garlic
>2 tablespoons chopped fresh sage leaves, or 2 teaspoons
>   rubbed sage

>18 chicken wings

>2 tablespoons white sesame seeds

>2 tablespoons fresh coriander leaves

Mix together ingredients for marinade in a nonreactive baking dish. Add chicken wings and set aside in refrigerator to marinate several hours or up to 2 days.

Preheat oven to 425 degrees. Place wings with marinade in oven and bake 45 minutes, turning after every 15 minutes.

Heat a small skillet, add sesame seeds, and toast over high heat, stirring constantly until seeds pop and turn golden. Sprinkle over chicken wings. Garnish with fresh coriander leaves.

CHICKEN DRUMMETTES:

>12 chicken wings

>1 tablespoon dry mustard
>1 tablespoon cayenne
>1 tablespoon black pepper
>1 tablespoon fresh thyme leaves, or 1 teaspoon dried

1½ cups flour

8 cups peanut oil

Remove tips from chicken wings and reserve for stock. Sever wings at "elbow" joints, to wind up with 24 pieces. Cut through skin and meat around the narrow end of each shoulder end (tibia) piece. Push meat up along bone and form into a ball at top end. Make an incision from bottom almost to the top between small bones of each middle joint (fibula) piece. With knife and fingers, remove small bone. Push meat up to the end along remaining bone and form into a ball. The sharper the knife, the easier this operation. Toss drummettes with dry mustard, cayenne, black pepper, and thyme. Set aside.

Place flour in a bowl or large bag. Add prepared wing pieces, a few at a time, and toss to coat.

In a 10 to 12 inch pot or skillet, heat oil until just starting to smoke. Shake excess flour off drummettes and fry in four batches 12 to 15 minutes, turning once. Remove to paper toweling and salt lightly.

Serve warm, accompanied with **Cumberland sauce** (see page 166) for dipping.

DEEP FRIED SQUID GREMOLATA

Whitebait or fresh small anchovies, rinsed and not gutted, may be used just as well for this Italian deep fried savory with the simple and fresh tasting gremolata garnish.

────────────── Cocktail savories for 6 ──────────────

3 pounds very fresh squid

6 cups peanut oil

2 cups flour

juice of 2 lemons
salt
pepper

For the gremolata:
> **grated rind of 6 lemons, chopped**
> **3 cloves garlic, minced**
> **½ cup chopped parsley**

Prepare squid as in recipe for **squid with peppers** (see page 225). Place prepared squid in a colander, rinse lightly, and place colander in a bowl large enough to hold it. Let squid drain in refrigerator several hours or overnight.

To fry squid, heat oil in a deep pot. Pat squid dry on paper toweling, then toss with flour. Deep fry in several batches, removing each batch to paper toweling. When all are cooked, place in a bowl and toss with lemon juice and salt and pepper to taste. In a small bowl, mix together ingredients for *gremolata*, add *gremolata* to bowl with squid, toss again. Serve warm or cold.

VEAL MEATBALLS
WITH DILL CREAM

For 24 meatballs, 2 to 3 ounces each

For grinding:

2 pounds veal bottom or stew meat
2 garlic cloves, peeled
1 onion, peeled
⅓ pound fatback

1 cup bread crumbs soaked in ½ cup milk
3 eggs
¾ cup chopped fresh parsley
¼ cup chopped fresh dill
1½ cups grated Parmesan cheese
1 teaspoon salt
½ teaspoon black pepper

4 tablespoons butter
flour

2 cups heavy cream
1 cup sour cream
2 tablespoons chopped fresh dill

2 tablespoons chopped fresh dill

Using the small plate, grind veal, garlic, onion, and fatback. Or purchase already ground veal and mince the garlic, onion, and fatback. With hands, thoroughly mix ground ingredients, bread crumbs, milk, eggs, herbs, cheese, and salt and pepper. Form into meatballs each about 1½ inches in diameter.

Preheat oven to 375 degrees. Melt butter in a skillet. Lightly flour meatballs and sauté them 3 to 5 minutes, until browned. Remove meatballs to a baking dish as you go. In a small bowl, stir cream into sour cream, then mix in dill. Pour over meatballs in the baking dish. Bake 20 minutes, or until an instant reading meat thermometer registers 160 degrees.

Serve sprinkled with more dill.

GNOCCHI WITH SWEET BUTTER
AND FRESH BASIL

_____ For 6 gnocchi, each about 6 inches long _____
and 1½ inches in diameter

For the dough:

>2 pounds russet potatoes
>2 cups unbleached all purpose white flour
>1½ teaspoons salt
>2 egg yolks
>2 tablespoons melted butter

For the filling:

>1 pound fresh spinach, leaves cut crosswise into ¼ inch
>   strips, stems chopped fine
>¾ cup ricotta cheese, drained
>½ cup grated Parmesan cheese, about 2 ounces
>½ teaspoon freshly grated nutmeg
>¼ teaspoon black pepper
>pinch of salt

For the garnish:

>shredded basil leaves
>1 cup sweet butter, melted and skimmed

Place potatoes in a large pot, cover with water by 3 inches, bring to a boil, and cook 35 minutes, or until quite done. Fork should easily pierce to center, but not as easily as for a baked potato. Drain and cool in a colander about 15 minutes. Peel. Place potatoes in a large skillet without any oil and dry over low heat 30 minutes, turning frequently. Set aside until cool enough to handle.

To prepare dough, first peel off skin formed on dried potatoes, then place potatoes in a large bowl and mash thoroughly with a fork. Or use a potato ricer, and rice into a large bowl. Add flour and salt to bowl, make

255

a well in the center, and place egg yolks in well. With hands, work dry ingredients together with egg yolks. A little at a time, incorporate melted butter into dough. Place dough on a floured surface and knead 10 minutes. Set aside to rest 30 minutes.

To prepare filling, wash spinach twice in plenty of cold water. Lift out into a colander and drain 5 minutes. Place in a nonreactive pot and stir over medium heat until completely wilted. Drain in a colander until cool enough to handle. Squeeze dry with hands, wrap in a cloth towel, and squeeze dry again. Mince with a chef's knife or purée in a food processor. Mix in remaining filling ingredients and adjust seasoning. Set aside.

To prepare gnocchi, divide dough into 6 balls. On a floured board, roll out each ball into a 2 inch circle ¼ inch thick. Place ¼ cup filling down the center, roll up, and seal edge with water. Wrap each roll in a cheesecloth square and tie ends with string. Set aside. Gnocchi may be refrigerated overnight.

To cook, bring a large pot of water to a boil. Drop in gnocchi and simmer 20 minutes. Add 5 minutes if they have been refrigerated. Remove to a colander or strainer and let dry 10 minutes before unwrapping.

To serve, unwrap, cut each gnocchi into six rounds, arrange on a plate with centers exposed, sprinkle shredded fresh basil over top and pour melted butter over all. Accompany with a bowl of Parmesan cheese, freshly grated on the large holes of a hand grater.

MUSHROOM PIE

This is an adaptation of an Eastern European Seder dish. Serve with sherry as a first course or cocktail savory.

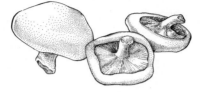

_____ For one 9 inch covered pie or _____
20 little tartlets

1 pound fresh mushrooms, including ¼ pound shiitake,
    if possible

4 tablespoons butter
1 small onion, chopped fine
1 teaspoon Hungarian paprika
1 teaspoon chopped fresh thyme leaves, or pinch of
    dried
¼ teaspoon cayenne
½ teaspoon salt
1½ tablespoons lemon juice
1 tablespoon Amontillado sherry
1½ tablespoons flour

1 pound pastry dough (see page 161), make a double
    batch

1 egg yolk
1 teaspoon milk, half and half, or cream

To prepare mushrooms, wipe clean with paper or cloth toweling. Trim stem ends of regular mushrooms. Trim off stems of shiitake, which are too tough for this dish, and reserve for soup stock. Mince mushrooms with a chef's knife; a food processor will mash the mushrooms and the texture will not be as pleasing.

To prepare filling, melt butter in a nonreactive skillet. When foaming, add onion and sauté over medium low heat until translucent. Add mushrooms, paprika, thyme, cayenne, and salt. Raise heat to medium high and cook 5 minutes. Add lemon juice and sherry and continue cooking until juices are mostly evaporated, 10 to 15 minutes. Stir occasionally. Sprinkle flour over the surface and stir to combine well. Cook 5 minutes longer, until mixture thickens. Remove from heat and cool completely before filling pie. Mushroom filling will keep refrigerated up to 5 days.

To prepare a covered pie, preheat oven to 425 degrees. Line a 9 inch pie dish or tart ring using ½ pound of the pastry. Prick bottom with a fork and bake 4 minutes. Prick bottom again and push up edges if necessary. Bake 6 minutes more. Remove and cool to room temperature.

Roll ¼ pound (half of remaining) pastry into a circle large enough to overlap edges of pie dish by 1 inch. Use last ¼ pound of pastry for another purpose. Fill cooled shell with cooled filling, top with pastry round, and pinch into decorative edge to seal. Mix egg yolk with milk, half and half, or cream and brush on top of pie. Make three or four slits in top of pie to allow steam to escape. Bake 30 to 35 minutes, until crust is golden.

To prepare hand pies, divide pastry in half and roll one half into a large circle about 13 inches in diameter. Press or cut out rounds approximately 3½ inches in diameter. Place 1½ tablespoons mushroom filling in the center of each and fold over to form half circles. Brush one edge of each circle with water, then press edges together with a fork to seal. Place on a baking sheet. Repeat with second half of dough. Glaze with egg wash as described and bake 20 minutes, until golden. Hand pies may be prepared in advance and frozen, unglazed, up to 1 week. Defrost and glaze before baking.

ARMENIAN LAMB PIZZAS

Armenian lamb pizza, called lahmejoun, *are thin crusted, crackerlike pizzas rather than deep dish, bready type pizzas. The traditional Eastern Mediterranean lamb topping is unusual and delicious, but the dough is suitable for numerous whimsical variations. Try, for instance, thin slices of Fontina cheese spread with shredded leeks first wilted in a little olive oil and lightly sprinkled with fresh thyme leaves and balsamic vinegar before popping into the oven.*

——————————— For 18 pizzas, 5 to 6 inches in diameter ———————————

For the dough:

　　1 tablespoon active dry yeast
　　3 tablespoons warm water
　　¾ cup lukewarm water
　　1 teaspoon salt
　　1 teaspoon sugar
　　3 tablespoons olive oil
　　2½ cups sifted unbleached all purpose white flour

For the topping:

　　1 pound ground lamb, preferably lamb shoulder
　　1 cup finely chopped green bell pepper, about 2 medium
　　　　size peppers
　　1 cup finely chopped onion, about 1½ medium size onions
　　1½ pounds fresh tomatoes, peeled, seeded, finely
　　　　chopped, and drained, or 1 can (28 ounces) Italian
　　　　plum tomatoes, drained and chopped fine
　　5 tablespoons rich tomato paste
　　¾ cup finely chopped parsley
　　1 tablespoon chopped fresh oregano leaves, or 1 teaspoon dried
　　½ teaspoon ground allspice
　　½ teaspoon paprika
　　¼ teaspoon cayenne
　　½ teaspoon black pepper
　　2 teaspoons salt

259
Savories

To make the dough, dissolve the yeast in 3 tablespoons warm water and let sit 15 minutes. Stir in ¾ cup water, the salt, sugar, and olive oil, then add sifted flour. Blend well, adding a little more flour or water to make a stiff dough. Knead with a mixer 5 minutes or with hands on a floured board 10 minutes, until dough is elastic and shiny, but remains soft. Place in a bowl rubbed with olive oil, rub olive oil over the surface of dough, cover with a towel, and set in a warm place to rise 1½ hours, or until doubled in size.

To make meat topping, place ingredients in a large bowl and mix together with hands. Set aside.

When dough has doubled in volume, turn out onto a well floured surface and cut into 18 equal portions. Roll each to form a small ball, then roll balls in flour to coat. Place 2 inches apart on a floured surface and cover first with a dry towel and then with a wet towel. Let rest 15 minutes.

Preheat oven to 475 degrees. Roll each dough ball into a 5 inch circle and place on a baking sheet. With fingers, evenly spread 2½ to 3 tablespoons meat mixture over top of each pizza. Do not use much more meat mixture or pizza will be soggy. Bake in the bottom of the oven 6 minutes, and then in the top of the oven 6 to 8 minutes, until edges and bottoms of crusts begin to turn golden.

Armenian lamb pizza may be served hot or cold. They are particularly good served hot with melted butter spread over the top. To store, pack in twos, placed face to face, and wrap in plastic. May be refrigerated up to 3 days or frozen up to 3 weeks. Reheat on a baking sheet in a 400 degree oven.

PICKLED CHERRIES

A specialty of southwest France, piquant and sweet pickled cherries make a perfect accompaniment for the charcuterie and cassoulets which are also a specialty of that region. Here are two versions. One, with tarragon vinegar, is more traditional and tarter. The other makes innovative use of the dense, almost smoky flavor of balsamic vinegar. The cherry season is short, so you should be poised to purchase at the moment when the price is not too outrageous and the cherries are good. Old recipes recommend using underripe or sour cherries, but we prefer the flavor of ripe sweet cherries and reduce the sugar in the pickling brine accordingly.

--- For 3 quarts ---

4 pounds unbruised ripe cherries

Pickle for Cherries I:

> **5 cups tarragon vinegar**
> **1 cup white vinegar**
> **2 cups sugar**
> **2 cardamom pods, cracked to release seeds**
> **4 cloves**

Pickle for Cherries II:

> **6 cups balsamic vinegar**
> **1 cup sugar**
> **2 bay leaves**
> **2 cloves**

Place ingredients for pickling in a nonreactive pot and bring to a boil. Remove and cool to tepid.

Wash cherries. Place them, with stems intact, in two clean and dry quart jars with screw top or rubber gasket seal lids. When it is tepid, pour pickle over cherries, cover, and age in a cool, dark place 3 weeks. Will keep indefinitely.

SWEETS

RICK'S MINCEMEAT

Rick's meaty, spicy, and not too sweet mincemeat pie is like that one fruitcake you've eaten, or just wondered about, which could elicit the aha! response; "That's what the taste is supposed to be about." We make ours early, in October, when thoughts turn to the changing season and coming Winter, so there is time for the mincemeat to age and mellow for holiday pies.

────────────────────── For about 2 gallons ──────────────────────

5 pounds beef shank with marrow

1 beef heart, about 2½ pounds, cut into ¼ inch dice
1½ pounds suet, chopped
1 pound dried currants
1 pound golden raisins
½ pound citron, chopped
2 pounds candied citrus peel (see page 277), chopped
2 cups dark molasses
1 pound brown sugar
1 quart sparkling cider, preferably French

3 pounds Pippin, Granny Smith, or other tart apples,
    cored and cut into ½ inch dice
2 quinces, cored and cut into ½ inch dice
1 tablespoon ground mace
2 teaspoons ground cinnamon
2 teaspoons grated nutmeg
2 teaspoons ground allspice
2 tablespoons white pepper
1 fifth brandy

Place beef shanks on a baking sheet and roast in a 350 degree oven 30 minutes. When done, remove and cool enough to handle. Cut meat into ¼ inch dice, remove marrow, and place both in a large pot.

Add heart, suet, currants, raisins, citron, candied citrus peels, molasses, brown sugar, and cider to the pot. Set over medium low heat and bring to a boil, stirring frequently. Cook while preparing apples and quinces.

Add apples and quinces, along with spices and brandy, to the pot. Place pot on a stovetop trivet and simmer 3 hours, stirring frequently. Remove from heat, cool, and pack into storage containers.

Refrigerate up to 1 year—mincemeat improves with age. Two cups will fill a 9 inch piecrust.

MARROW PIE

This intriguing concoction, an adaptation of a Toulouse-Lautrec flattery, is reminiscent of medieval cookery, which abounds with recipes combining meat with sweets, spices, and milk. Our version tones down the sugar and cinnamon to suit the contemporary taste. Marrow pie is a very rich accompaniment to roast game, turkey, or goose dishes.

--- For an 11 inch pie ---

5 pounds beef marrow bones, including 1 beef shank

¾ pound pastry dough (see page 161)

1 tablespoon butter

2 large eggs
1 cup sugar
1½ cups half and half
½ teaspoon ground cinnamon

Preheat oven to 375 degrees. Place marrow bones and beef shank on a baking sheet and bake 30 minutes. Remove. When cool enough to handle, spoon marrow out of centers of bones. Roughly chop meat, including any fat.

Roll out pastry and line a 12 inch pie or tart pan. Prick bottom with fork tines and place pastry in the oven. After 5 minutes, push up sides of dough if falling down and push down bottom if puffing up. Bake 5 to 7 minutes, until pastry is just beginning to turn golden. Remove from oven and set aside to cool. Reduce oven heat to 325 degrees.

Heat butter in a small saucepan until foaming. Stir in marrow and chopped meat and remove from heat. Set aside.

In a medium size bowl, beat eggs lightly. Add sugar and beat until color lightens. Whisk in half and half and cinnamon. Stir in marrow and meat. Fill the prebaked pastry shell. Place in the oven and bake 40 to 50 minutes, until a knife inserted in the center comes out clean. Serve right away.

BREAD PUDDING

2 large or 3 medium apples, Golden Delicious or
    Granny Smith
1/4 pound butter
1/3 teaspoon ground allspice

6 large eggs
1 quart milk
1 cup sugar
1 1/2 teaspoons whiskey or rum (optional)

1 loaf of stale French bread, cut into 1 inch cubes,
    about 6 cups

Preheat oven to 350 degrees. Halve and core apples without peeling. Cut halves into halves again then slice crosswise 1/8 inch thick. In a skillet, melt butter until foaming, add apples and allspice, and sauté 5 minutes to soften apples without browning.

In a large bowl, beat eggs lightly. Beat in milk, sugar, and liquor if you are using it. Stir in softened apples then the cubed bread. Pour into a 2 quart glass or ceramic baking terrine or soufflé mold. Bake 55 minutes, or until top is quite golden and puffed up and custard is set.

POPPY SEED CAKE

—————————— For a 3 quart bundt pan ——————————

1³/₄ cups granulated sugar
4 large eggs

1¹/₂ cups peanut, light olive, or walnut oil

3 cups unbleached all purpose white flour
1¹/₂ teaspoons baking soda
¹/₂ teaspoon salt

1¹/₂ cups half and half

1 cup pulverized or finely chopped walnuts
4 tablespoons poppy seeds

Preheat oven to 350 degrees. Grease and flour a 3 quart bundt pan. Cream sugar and eggs together until light and fluffy. Beat in oil. Sift together flour, baking soda, and salt. Add to batter alternately with half and half.

Place chopped walnuts in an ungreased skillet, set over medium heat, and stir to toast, until nuts are turning brown and a nutty aroma is released. Stir walnuts and poppy seeds into the batter and pour the batter into the prepared bundt pan. Bake 1 hour and 10 minutes, until a knife inserted in the center comes out clean.

Let the cake rest 15 minutes, then unmold and let it rest in the inverted position 1 hour. Poppy seed cake will keep wrapped in plastic and refrigerated up to 1 week.

CURRANT CAKE

—————————————— For about 2½ pounds currant cake ——————————————

¾ pound dried currants

½ pound unsalted butter, softened to room temperature
1 cup granulated sugar

4 large eggs
½ teaspoon grated mace
1 teaspoon vanilla extract

2 cups unbleached all purpose white flour, measured
   after sifting

Immerse currants in cold water and let them soak 5 minutes. Drain in a colander, and pat dry on paper toweling before using.

Preheat oven to 325 degrees. Grease and flour a 2 quart loaf pan or two 1 pound loaf pans.

Beat butter until white and fluffy. Slowly add 1 cup granulated sugar and beat until graininess disappears. Add eggs, one at a time, beating well after each addition. Mix in mace and vanilla. Add dried currants to batter and stir in. Add flour all at once and mix in without overbeating.

Pour batter into pans and bake 1 hour to 1 hour and 10 minutes, or slightly less if using two smaller pans, until a knife inserted in the center comes out clean. Remove from oven, turn out on a rack and cool. Wrap in plastic and refrigerate. Currant cake is best if aged 5 days before serving, and it will keep wrapped and refrigerated up to 2 months.

BISCOTTI

This recipe for ever popular biscotti is Ann's version, less sweet than many others, and enhanced with anise-flavored brandy, made by soaking anise seeds in brandy for several days. Biscotti are easy to make and will keep in an airtight container for some months. Dunked into Zinfandel wine, they make a perfect tea-time treat.

--- For approximately 50 cookies ---

1 cup nuts, almonds and hazelnuts or all almonds

3 large eggs
¾ cup sugar

⅓ cup unsalted butter, melted and cooled to room temperature

grated rind of 1 lemon
1 tablespoon lemon juice
¼ teaspoon almond extract
1 tablespoon anise brandy or ½ teaspoon anise extract
½ cup dried currants or raisins
½ cup candied citrus peel (see page 277), made with lemon, cut into ¼ inch dice

3 cups unbleached all purpose white flour
1 teaspoon baking powder
⅛ teaspoon salt

Use a chef's knife or food processor to chop nuts well without pulverizing. Place chopped nuts in an ungreased skillet and stir over medium high heat until browned. Set aside.

Beat eggs until beginning to thicken, about 2 minutes. Add sugar and beat until mixture is pale yellow. Stir in butter, without including sediment. Stir in lemon rind, lemon juice, almond and anise flavorings, currants or raisins, and candied lemon peel. Add the toasted nuts and mix in.

Sift flour, baking powder, and salt over batter, then stir in. Dough will be stiff.

To cook, preheat oven to 350 degrees. Butter and flour a baking sheet. Divide dough into four parts. Lightly flour hands and roll each part into a 12 inch long cylinder 2 inches in diameter. Place on the baking sheet and bake 20 to 25 minutes, until loaves are beginning to turn golden. Remove from oven and allow to cool 25 minutes.

Cut the loaves into ½ to ¾ inch wide slices at a 45 degree angle. Lay slices flat on the baking sheet, return to the oven and toast 5 to 8 minutes on each side until light brown.

Remove from oven, cool completely, then store in an airtight tin, glass, or plastic container.

PEPPERNUT COOKIES

These traditional Christmas cookies, familiarly called Pfeffer-
nüsse in German, are like the fourth century Roman sweets
described by Apicius, which happily mix nuts, honey (since they
lacked sugar in those times), sweet spices, and pepper. Peppernut
cookies are best after 5 days, and improve with age. A con-
tainerful misplaced in the Christmas rush one year tasted delicious
in February!

―――――――――――――― For 170 to 175 cookies ――――――――――――――

1 pound unsalted butter, softened to room temperature
2½ cups granulated sugar

1 cup heavy cream
1 tablespoon ground ginger
2 teaspoons ground cinnamon
1 teaspoon ground cardamom
2 teaspoons freshly ground black pepper
½ cup finely chopped toasted walnuts

2 teaspoons baking soda
1½ tablespoons heavy cream

1 teaspoon baking powder
6¾ cups, 2 pounds, unbleached all purpose white flour
powdered sugar, for coating cookies

Cream butter until light and fluffy. Slowly beat in sugar. Mix
in 1 cup cream, the ginger, cinnamon, cardamom, black pepper, and
walnuts. Mix baking soda with remaining cream then add to batter. Sift
baking powder and flour into batter and blend together without overmixing.

Preheat oven to 325 degrees. Roll dough into 1 inch diameter balls.
Place on baking sheets, and bake 15 to 20 minutes, until pale brown on
underside. Cool, then sprinkle with sifted powdered sugar. Store unrefrigerated in airtight containers.

ALMOND CRESCENTS

¾ pound unsalted butter, softened to room temperature
¾ cup granulated sugar
1¾ cups toasted, then pulverized or finely chopped
   blanched almonds
1½ teaspoons vanilla extract
3½ cups unbleached all purpose white flour

½ cup powdered sugar

Cream butter in a food processor or with an electric mixer. Add granulated sugar and beat in. Add almonds, vanilla, and flour and beat in. Mixture should not be too buttery; add more flour if necessary. Press dough firmly and evenly into a 10 by 12 inch pan and refrigerate until firm, about 45 minutes.

Preheat oven to 350 degrees. Cut dough lengthwise into ¾ inch wide strips, then slice strips into 3 inch long pieces. With floured fingers, pinch each piece into a crescent shape, pushing toward middle to keep from breaking. Place on an ungreased baking sheet and bake 12 to 15 minutes, until barely browned on bottoms. Remove and cool.

Sprinkle with sifted powdered sugar. Store out of refrigerator in an airtight container. Almond crescents are a bit delicate and do not keep well beyond 4 or 5 days.

PASTINE DI POLENTA

For about 10 dozen cookies

1 cup yellow cornmeal
1 cup sieved unbleached all purpose white flour
½ cup powdered sugar
1 tablespoon baking powder
grated rind of 1 lemon

1 cup pulverized or very finely chopped almonds
⅓ cup finely chopped candied citrus peel (see page 277)
    or grated rind of 2 medium oranges

½ pound unsalted butter, softened to room temperature

2 large eggs, slightly beaten
1 tablespoon orange juice
½ teaspoon almond extract

extra cornmeal and flour for kneading

powdered sugar

Mix together cornmeal, flour, sugar, baking powder, and lemon rind. Mix in almonds and candied citrus peel. Add butter, cut into small pieces, and blend with fingers as for making pastry. Make a well in the center and add eggs, orange juice, and almond extract. Mix in, gather up dough, and place on a counter dusted with cornmeal and flour. Knead lightly, about 2 minutes, then form into one lump. Wrap and chill 30 minutes.

Preheat oven to 375 degrees. Grease and flour baking sheets.

Cut and press dough into egg size pieces, dust bottoms with cornmeal and place on baking sheets. Bake 12 to 15 minutes, until barely golden. Remove, cool, and sprinkle with sifted powdered sugar. Store, unrefrigerated, in an airtight container up to several weeks.

ITALIAN MERINGUES

Snowy white and crunchy Italian style meringues made with home candied citrus peel make virtuous use of leftover egg whites. Vary the recipe by adding an equal amount of grated chocolate or finely chopped and toasted almonds or hazelnuts in place of the candied citrus peel.

——————————— For 18 meringue cookies ———————————

2 cups sugar
²/₃ cup water

¾ cup egg whites, about 6, at room temperature

¾ cup candied citrus peel (recipe follows), diced

In a heavy saucepan, combine sugar and water and set over medium high heat. Swirl pan to mix, but do not stir. Reduce heat to maintain a slow simmer and cook to the soft ball stage, or until a candy thermometer registers 238 degrees.

Beat egg whites until stiff. When sugar syrup is ready, beat egg whites again, then beat in boiling syrup until incorporated. Continue beating 8 to 10 minutes, until mixture is cool and shiny. Cooling may be hastened by setting bowl into cool water.

Preheat oven to 200 to 225 degrees. Butter and flour two baking sheets or line them with brown paper.

Add diced citrus peel to meringue batter and stir in. Drop meringues onto baking sheets by spoonsful, then flatten each. Place in the oven and bake 45 minutes to 1 hour, until cookies are dry but not brown. Remove from oven and loosen from the baking sheet while still warm. Stored in airtight containers out of direct light, meringues will keep up to 1 week.

CANDIED CITRUS PEEL:

3 cups sugar
2 cups water
juice of 1 lemon

rind of 12 lemons, Meyer lemons especially,
    or 8 medium oranges, or a mixture

Place sugar, water, and lemon juice in a medium size nonreactive pot and bring to a boil over medium high heat. Cook over medium heat 15 minutes, until syrup is slightly thickened.

Pare off ends of citrus fruits, then halve and juice them. Reserve juice for another purpose. Cut each half into quarters.

Add citrus peel to syrup and continue simmering 30 minutes. Remove from heat and cool. Lift peels out of syrup and store in a covered container in the refrigerator. Reserve syrup for other uses. Candied citrus peels will keep refrigerated several months. Makes about 4 cups.

MADELEINES

There are all kinds of madeleines in the world, from homemade
to commercially distributed, some soft, some harder. This version
is of true Proustian splendor, a tea cake rather than a cookie,
the taste of which is delicately balanced between sweet and
buttery. The traditional shell shape obtained by baking the cookies
in a madeleine mold is, at least subjectively, essential to the
flavor.

For 32 madeleines

½ pound unsalted butter

1¼ cups sugar
5 large eggs

butter and flour for molds

1¾ cups sieved unbleached all purpose white flour
pinch of salt
grated rind of 1 lemon
1 tablespoon lemon juice
1 teaspoon vanilla extract

Heat butter until melted and set aside to cool. In the top pan
of a double boiler, or in a bowl set over a pot of boiling water, whisk
together sugar and eggs until slightly warm. Remove from heat and set
aside to cool while preparing other ingredients.

Preheat oven to 375 degrees. Butter and lightly flour madeleine molds.

Add flour, salt, lemon rind and juice, and vanilla to sugar and eggs.
Beat until smooth. Add melted butter, not including sediment, and blend
well. Spoon batter into madeleine molds to make them two thirds full.
Bake 16 to 17 minutes, until lightly golden and beginning to shrink from
edges. Remove and pry out gently. If baking in more than one batch,

wipe off residue, which can burn, then butter and flour molds for each additional batch. Run cool water over back of madeleine molds to cool between bakings.

Madeleines may be stored in an airtight tin or refrigerated in plastic wrap up to 1 week. Or store in freezer bags in the freezer up to 1 month.

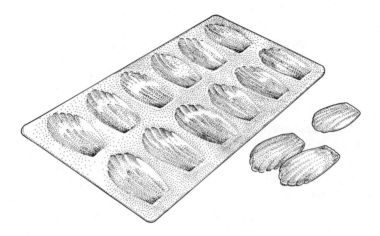

■ ■

SHORTBREAD

For 1 pound shortbread

⅔ cup unsalted butter, softened to room temperature
½ cup powdered sugar

1½ cups plus 2 tablespoons unbleached all purpose
    white flour, measured after sifting
½ teaspoon salt

Preheat oven to 325 degrees. Line an ungreased 8 inch pie dish with wax paper.

Cream butter and sugar together until light yellow and fluffy. Sift flour and salt together and add to sugar and butter. Blend well. Pat batter firmly into the lined pie dish. With a sharp-pronged fork, prick deeply in lines to mark off breaking places.

Place in the oven and bake 45 minutes, or until light golden and beginning to shrink from pan. Remove and cool on a rack, then wrap in plastic wrap or place in an airtight tin. Age 5 days before cutting. Will keep several weeks.

■ ■

PEARS IN SAUTERNES

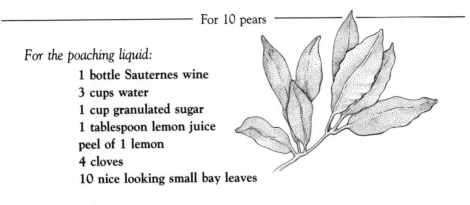

──────────────── For 10 pears ────────────

For the poaching liquid:

- 1 bottle Sauternes wine
- 3 cups water
- 1 cup granulated sugar
- 1 tablespoon lemon juice
- peel of 1 lemon
- 4 cloves
- 10 nice looking small bay leaves

10 Comice, French Butter, or other firm, ripe pears

Place ingredients for poaching liquid in a medium size non-reactive pot just large enough to hold 5 pears. Bring to a boil, reduce heat to medium, and barely simmer 10 minutes.

Carefully peel 5 pears to maintain a nice shape, leaving stems intact. Drop into the poaching liquid and simmer 10 to 15 minutes, depending on how ripe pears are, until flesh barely gives when pushed. Turn frequently to poach evenly. Remove to a bowl or deep dish large enough to hold 10 pears. Peel and poach remaining 5 pears. Add pears and bay leaves to the first batch of pears. Continue cooking the liquid 15 minutes. Cool poaching liquid then pour over pears. Refrigerate to chill completely.

To serve, place pears in a deep serving dish, spoon syrup over top, and arrange a bay leaf next to each stem to resemble a leaf.

STRAWBERRIES STEWED WITH THYME
AND RED WINE

Bright red strawberries, halved and barely poached in a slightly sweet aromatic sauce, make one of the prettiest fruit compotes. This is a versatile side dish, to serve at breakfast, for dessert, or with a bowl of fresh fromage blanc *for a satisfying snack any time.*

—————————————— For 1½ quarts compote ——————————————

3 cups strong red wine
½ cup granulated sugar
8 sprigs fresh thyme, or ½ teaspoon dried

4 baskets fresh strawberries

2 sprigs fresh thyme or fresh mint

Place wine, sugar, and 8 sprigs of thyme in a medium size nonreactive pot and bring to a boil. Reduce heat to medium and cook 5 minutes.

Wash berries and sort into two piles: one of overripe and underripe berries, which should be about 1½ baskets' worth, and the second of just right berries. Hull and halve them all and add overripe and underripe berries to the pot. Set the pot on a metal stovetop trivet over medium low heat and cook without disturbing 1 hour. Set aside remaining berries in refrigerator.

Off the heat, remove cooked fruit from liquid and push through a fine sieve, or purée in a blender or food processor. Return, pulp and all, to pot. Stir in reserved strawberries, tuck in 2 sprigs of fresh thyme or fresh mint, stir, and allow berries to cool in the liquid 15 minutes. Chill. Strawberry compote will keep in the refrigerator several weeks.

FROMAGE BLANC:

2 quarts milk
1 cup plain yogurt
1 tablespoon lemon juice

Slowly bring milk to a boil. Gently whisk yogurt until smooth, then add to milk and stir. Remove from heat and cool to tepid. Add lemon juice and let rest 1 hour more.

Set a strainer lined with cheesecloth or other loose weave cloth in a bowl. Pour milk mixture into the strainer and let drain 3 hours. Chill. Thin the cheese with a little cream before serving if desired.

Note: Whey drained off *fromage blanc* and collected in a bowl contains lactic acid, which is a tenderizing agent. Reserve it to make a Middle Eastern style roast chicken; tenderize chicken by marinating overnight in whey mixed with 1 cup yogurt and some good curry powder.

■ ■

CHRISTINE'S CITRUS AND MINT SHERBET

For 6, about 1½ quarts sherbet

1 cup superfine granulated sugar
2 cups water
grated rind of 1 lemon
grated rind of 1 orange

1½ cups packed fresh mint leaves

1 cup orange juice, with pulp
1 cup lime juice

2 egg whites

Place sugar, water, and grated rinds in a medium size pot and bring to a boil. Reduce heat to medium and simmer 5 minutes. Pour syrup over mint sprigs in a heatproof bowl and let steep 15 minutes.

Strain liquid into a 1½ quart container suitable for the freezer, pressing down on mint leaves. Stir in orange and lime juices. Freeze. When almost frozen solid, 4 to 6 hours, break up into slush with an electric mixer.

Beat egg whites until soft peaks form. Fold into the citrus and mint slush, one third at a time. Refreeze until almost set, then beat until smooth. Repeat when almost set again, smooth top, and allow to freeze until set. Remove from freezer 30 minutes before serving.

BARBARA'S CHOCOLATE TRUFFLES

Chocolate truffles are a cinch to make and a delightful treat to everyone. The trick is to use good chocolate: baker's coating or candy making chocolate both handle well. Truffles may be made weeks in advance of using and stored in the freezer without any damage to the taste or texture.

——————————————— For approximately 80 truffles ———————————————

1 pound semisweet baking chocolate

¾ cup pulverized blanched almonds

½ pound unsalted butter, softened to room temperature

6 egg yolks
3 tablespoons liqueur such as Grand Marnier or Kahlua, or rum

¾ cup powdered cocoa

Grate semisweet chocolate in a food processor or blender, or with a hand grater. Put into a mixing bowl and place in a 130 degree oven until just melted but still holding shape in center, about 15 minutes.

Place pulverized almonds in an ungreased skillet and stir over medium heat until toasted. Set aside.

Remove chocolate from oven and beat in butter until incorporated. Beat in egg yolks, then beat in liqueur or rum. Add toasted almonds and blend well. Cover and refrigerate 3 hours or overnight.

To finish, have ready two baking sheets, one with a thick layer of powdered cocoa.

Using a soup spoon, scrape a spoonful off the top of the chocolate, roll into a ball between palms, and drop onto the baking sheet with cocoa. When baking sheet is full, shake to coat truffles. Coat fingers with cocoa and remove truffles to clean baking sheet. Refrigerate to set. Store in plastic storage bags in the refrigerator or freezer.

I hope it is somewhat better than whim at last,
but we cannot spend the day in explanation.

—Ralph Waldo Emerson

BIBLIOGRAPHY

Auge, R., editor, *Cours Professionnels Artisanaux: Charcutier*, Volumes 1, 2, 3, Paris: Editions de l'Artisant Moderne

Baboian, Rose, *Armenian-American Cookbook*, Baboian, 1964

Chamberlain, Samuel, *Bouquet de France*, New Edition, New York: Gourmet, 1966

Child, Julia, and Beck, Simone, *Mastering the Art of French Cooking*, Volumes 1 and 2, New York: Knopf, 1970

Child, Julia, *From Julia Child's Kitchen*, New York: Knopf, 1975

Courtine, Robert, *The Hundred Glories of French Cooking*, New York: Farrar, Straus, Giroux, 1971

Cruess, William V., *Home and Farm Food Preservation*, New York: Macmillan, 1925

Dali, Salvador, *Les Dîners de Gala*, New York: Felicie, 1973

David, Elizabeth, *Italian Food*, Baltimore: Penguin, 1963

——, *French Provincial Cooking*, New York: Harper and Row, 1962

——, *Spices, Salts, and Aromatics of the English Kitchen*, New York: Penguin, 1970

Desrosier, Norman W. and James N., *The Technology of Food Preservation*, Fourth Edition, Westport, Connecticut: AVI, 1977

Field, Michael, *Michael Field's Cooking School*, New York: Holt, Rinehart and Winston, 1965

Garland, Sarah, *The Complete Book of Herbs and Spices*, New York: Viking, 1979

Gerrard, Frank, *Sausage and Small Goods Production*, Fourth Edition, London: Leonard Hill, 1959

Gewanter, Vera, *A Passion for Vegetables*, New York: Viking, 1980

Grigson, Jane, *The Art of Charcuterie and French Pork Cookery*, New York: Knopf, 1965

————, *Jane Grigson's Fruit Book*, New York: Atheneum, 1982

————, *Jane Grigson's Vegetable Book*, New York: Penguin, 1981

Hawthorne, Ronald; Kowallis, Winifred; and York, George, *Snails as Food*, University of California, Leaflet 2222, 1975

Hazan, Marcella, *The Classic Italian Cookbook*, New York: Knopf, 1976

Hickey, John C., and Brant, Dr. A. Wade, *Sausage Maker's Handbook*

Hippisley Coxe, Antony, and Hippisley Coxe, Araminta, *The Book of the Sausage*, London: Pan, 1978

Hom, Ken, with Harvey Steiman, *Chinese Technique*, New York: Simon and Schuster, 1981

Innes, Jocasta, *Your Country Kitchen*, Charlotte, Vermont: Garden Way, 1982

Johnston, Mireille, *Cuisine of the Sun*, New York: Random House, 1976

Junior League of Lafayette, *Talk About Good II*, Lafayette, Louisiana: Junior League of Lafayette, 1979

Lasnet de Lanty, Henriette, *Conserves Familiales*, Paris: Flammarion, 1965

————, *La Charcuterie à la Campagne*, Paris: La Maison Rustique, 1975

Lobel, Leon and Stanley, *All About Meat*, New York and London: Harcourt Brace Jovanovich, 1975

McClane, A. J., *The Encyclopedia of Fish Cookery*, New York: Holt, Rinehart and Winston, 1977

Montagne, Prosper, *Larousse Gastronomique*, New York: Crown, 1961

Morton Salt Company, *Home Meat Curing*, Chicago: Morton Salt Company

Oliver, Raymond, *La Cuisine*, New York: Tudor, 1969

Olney, Richard, *Simple French Food*, New York: Atheneum, 1977

————, editor, *The Good Cook/Techniques and Recipes: Pork*, Alexandria, Virginia: Time Life Books, 1980

————, editor, *The Good Cook/Techniques and Recipes: Preserving*, Alexandria, Virginia: Time Life Books, 1981

————, editor, *The Good Cook/Techniques and Recipes: Terrines, Pâtés and Galantines*, Alexandria, Virginia: Time Life Books, 1982

Pépin, Jacques, *La Technique*, New York: Quadrangle/The New York Times Book Company, 1976

Prudhomme, Paul, *Chef Paul Prudhomme's Louisiana Kitchen*, New York: William Morrow, 1984

Revel, Jean-François, *Culture and Cuisine*, New York: Da Capo, 1984

Root, Waverly, *Food*, New York: Simon and Schuster, 1980

Sokolov, Raymond, *Fading Feast*, New York: Farrar, Straus, Giroux, 1981

Toulouse-Lautrec, Henri de, and Joyant, Maurice, *The Art of Cuisine*, New York: Crescent, 1966

Wolfert, Paula, *The Cooking of South West France*, New York: Dial Press, 1983

INDEX

297

298